A ROOM IN MOSCOW

A Room in Moscow

SALLY BELFRAGE

REYNAL & COMPANY

NEW YORK

Contents

For
Joe, Cheng, Cecil, André and Vladimir
—who have a lot in common

Foreword

ON MY TWENTY-FIRST BIRTHDAY the first sputnik was launched and I was travelling in a jet plane at the rate of 550 miles an hour. The future is mine, and my friends' in America, England, China, Russia, everywhere where the young are growing up and taking a first look at the world they have inherited.

Through a series of lucky accidents I have been able to see a lot of the world, and meet my contemporaries in the four countries which may have most influence over the future. It will be in their hands. Many of them are angry that it should be; that they, through no more than a simple accident of birth, in time and place, should have been bequeathed the responsibility of seeing that there actually is a future at all, by their elders who at times appear intent on destroying not only their enemies, but their friends, and even themselves. We think that mankind has fine possibilities, and that there is no reason why everything should not be possible for us. But we see our leaders frantically obscuring every issue, conducting minor revolutions over semantics, asserting 'our' right and 'their' wrong, creating unnecessary barriers and painting one side white and the other black, tearing people apart and from the happiness they could give one another, and generally indulging in the most grotesque hypocrisy. For what?

We like each other, and we hope we can avoid the disease.

1

Most of all, we want never to forget that we are all the same, and that even if we are divided by ideas, those ideas have fundamentally more in common than not. Each one is based on many of the same things, and we have plenty to do just to share what we can rather than concentrate on differences.

That jet was flying from China, where I had spent six weeks, to the USSR, where I lived for five months. I stayed there to try to discover the living realities beneath the symbols to which I, and all Westerners, had been exposed. I was unqualified to judge Russia's political system, its economic organization, or its institutional complex, but I did want to find out about the people who lived within the system. What was it like to live there? What did the Russians think of their society? What did they dream about? How happy were they? How socially adjusted? How much did they know about the rest of the world? Did they fear us? Could we get through to each other?

I found some of the answers, and came to understand a little about Russians. I want to write about them because so few in the West know anything about them as people, and so many in the West forget they even *are*, classing them instead into a symbolic lump which they either hate or love. But the Russians are not stereotyped or monotonous, and this attitude, in this world, is dangerous.

It is probably impossible to deal with as politically controversial a subject as this in an unpolitical way, and there inevitably seems to be some sort of explanation or apology needed at the start. First, because some of the Russians I knew were as passionately opposed to their government as others were passionately in favour, it is necessary to conceal the identity of them all. My views, too, can't be left out. When I went to Russia I fully believed myself capable of objectivity (as who does not), but this was not as true as I had hoped; I soon saw that I had carried my share of Western prejudices along. Living there, and having many of them cleared up, made me see things in a much more confident light.

1

The Party Spirit

BEING THE CHILD of a rebel is an unfortunate thing if one has tendencies in that direction anyway—because by going along with the rebellious parents one is in fact conforming. I was brought up in America by English dissenters. I appreciate them because without them my mind would never have developed out of the normal female groove; there would never have been any contradictions that required thought.

My parents travelled a great deal and eventually landed in Hollywood, where they were writers and where I was born. The Spanish Civil War made them political, and that decided everything. Later, in New York, my father began a left-wing newspaper, and both parents were subsequently deported back to England.

As a child I felt continually confused by all the clashing influences around me: my father and his beliefs, the others and theirs, and the fact that everyone could hate so much simply *because* of beliefs. The greatest value I got from that was a loathing of intolerance. But in the meantime I felt the conflict continually, from teachers in school who had a vast emotional hatred of me and my brother because our father's name was sometimes in the newspapers for the wrong reasons, and from boyfriends' mothers who threatened suicide if something wasn't done about me AT ONCE. I decided that nothing political was worth it, and that the important thing for me to do was to try to solve my own problems before I took on the world's. I didn't care what any of them thought, and just didn't think about it myself.

It didn't work out as I'd planned, because it couldn't. I was always too personally involved in the world's problems. But my particular method of rebellion, if it had to be that way, was to ally myself with neither side, and in the meantime to learn what I could of both.

I lived for two years in London after the deportations. Though I could have stayed in America, I preferred it that way because England was just the place to be unpolitical, and I had seen too much hysteria and hatred. No one got very excited about anything in England, which meant they avoided the worst abuses of excitement but also that it took quite a long time for anything to get done. What I liked was the freedom and tolerance, which I had never experienced so positively before. I didn't believe in anything, but no one held even that against me, and I was free to indulge in my special brand of escapism.

Then I heard about the Moscow Youth Festival. It was cheap, and I didn't know what to expect, and I could never resist bargains or surprises. I wanted more than anything to see what Russia was like. And someone hinted that if I signed up with the American delegation (I could have gone British, since I'm also British) there was a chance of being invited to China, which seemed the most interesting and exotic place I could think of. So altogether, there were several good reasons for going.

Not having a great deal of faith in the China idea, I packed enough for only three weeks of festival and embarked on a gruesome four-day train journey to Moscow. The only thing we had to pay was the fare from London to the Russian frontier and back, and that was a bargain because of the excruciating trains. I didn't think then that I would be spending a good part of the next two months on trains; this one was bad enough. For the first two days, seven Americans and I sat on benches like rocks looking at each other with eyes that got progressively blearier, having nowhere to sleep and no food but packed lunch boxes of salami and hard-boiled eggs. Roughing it. After that the trains improved, and across Germany and Poland there were baggage racks to sleep on in shifts.

The people on the train were almost all British except those in my compartment, and were a fascinating crew. They immediately seemed to sort out everyone according to accent and stuck together that way. Some of them were Oxford and Cambridge students out for an 'amusing' holiday, some intense London School of Economics type intellectuals, some school kids, some Communists. The Scots wore kilts and had bagpipes to show Moscow, and stopping at stations on the way they played and danced reels on the platforms. A couple of jazz bands and many guitarists accompanied rock 'n' rollers and folk singers, all to an audience of startled Germans, then Poles, then Russians. The journey was livened up by such people as the boy who brought a sack of thousands of I LIKE IKE buttons to trade with the Russians—visions of all those Muscovites wearing them and not knowing what they said— and one boy in the know who brought along a hammock that he attached to opposite ends of his compartment to get some sleep, except that everyone else wanted to use it too and gave him no peace.

We thought that we were exhausted and only semi-conscious by the time we reached Moscow, but that was nothing, nothing at all. In the next three weeks there was no choice but to forget about sleep, and people were transformed from moderately civilized human beings into brutes or sleep-walkers, depending on how they reacted—like being drunk, and the real you, and all that. Though they all had one thing in common by the end, and that was Asian flu.

There was the most wonderful fireworks excitement in Moscow! Arriving on a beautiful sunny day, we were met by thousands of cheering young people throwing flowers and shouting *Mir! Drouzhba!* (Peace! Friendship!) and driven through Moscow. Nothing seemed unusual after the crazy fantasy of being in Moscow that first day. It looked beautiful, with wide streets and green trees, and a sensation of space that I had never felt in a city of such size. Each building was decorated with banners and pictures, there was colour everywhere, and wherever you looked, people, waving and shouting and singing. The streets pulsated with movement and gaiety, all day long and far into the night.

We stayed in a hostel in the outskirts, five in a room, with fifteen or so interpreters. I saw only a few of them so was never quite sure how many there were. They were an indifferent lot, who detested Americans on principle and were models of inefficiency. After a long completely dense talk with one of them the first day, I felt I would never be able to make contact with these people; we couldn't seem to begin, proceed or end anywhere near each other.

The three weeks passed in a blur of activity, of exhibitions, mass celebrations, excursions, concerts, seminars, parties, shows, and *mir i drouzhba*. And the informal part as well—people from all countries arguing, discussing, collecting autographs and badges and making friends. It was simply marvellous. But it was difficult to get a clear idea of what Moscow was really like, and I decided quite soon to try to stay on afterwards.

I met a few Russians, but everything was so hectic. Always, when I walked a few yards down any street, Russians came up to me and spoke if they could, smiled and traded badges if they couldn't. The further I progressed the more Russians I collected—in the end a Pied Piper's procession of up to fifty people. Perhaps one could speak English, and he would be tormented to interpret for all the others who wanted to ask me questions. Everyone was eager and warm, and consumed with the desire to convey to me how much they loved me and wanted peace with my countries—either or both of them.

It was political, but in a human way far more effective than any organized campaigns or speeches could ever be. It taught everyone, microscopically, how alike all mankind is, how similar their language and dreams and instincts.

The 160 Americans there were unsponsored, disorganized, and a little pathetic compared to the rest and considering what they were supposed to represent. Being Americans they became political about it all right away and split into groups much the same as the English had with their accents. Most were there from curiosity and interest, some purely from political conviction or to make money journalistically, a few as lone crusaders for their America. Of these, one or two spent their days in Red Square reciting the UN report on Hungary to those who would listen. Another boy who was caught with a camera by the police climbing over a wall into a munitions factory, replied, when asked why, that he thought it was a short cut back to the hostel. They found him again a few days later in the same spot taking pictures. He wanted some souvenir snapshots, he said. A girl in my room hunted all and every day for Red Army soldiers, and one evening during a fair finally discovered a paradise of soldiers behind an enclosure in Gorky Park. She spent the night talking to them, 'getting material for a book'. She had a new idea, she said, that would save the world from all its folly and anxiety: none of the Red Army would fight, if you come right down to it—they were such nice men.

We were all kinds—chic ones from the east and drawly southerners, scientists, religious observers, bearded artists, representatives from the Parisian American set, students combining the festival with a tour of Europe. Few were terribly *American*, in the average sense, but I couldn't explain exactly what I mean by that. In terms of other delegations, anyway, they were a flop: everyone else sent musicians and dancers, good artists, actors, sportsmen and so on, while we had to make up for our utter lack of the professional touch with spirit, and that was pretty faltering some of the time.

The invitation to China did materialize, and included anyone who wanted to go. The group spent the last of its Moscow days considering and arguing. To go on the trip was against passport regulations and the American Embassy sent a man with letters to each of us from the State Department; still, all but a few of the fifty who had originally signed up decided to go ahead. The one phone for our use in the hostel corridor was booked solid with calls to parents. Shouts rang down the hall, as well as across the Atlantic: 'Please, Mom, be reasonable!' 'Father, I'm *not* a Communist!' Cables arrived —DON'T GO LOVE MOTHER—and some didn't. But forty-two went ahead. Quite a few were left-wingers, because they had been at the festival for that reason and happened to be able to take more time away from home; I don't know of any right-wingers who failed to go simply because of principle. Almost all, whatever their beliefs, disagreed with the State Department on the main issue. Freedom to travel is as basic as any other freedom, and all of us were very conscious of freedom, being in Moscow and finding ourselves involved in constant discussions on the subject with people from everywhere. No one even thought of restricting travel until fifty years ago, when tsarist Russia started issuing passports, and everyone else thought it rather quaint and peculiar. Then passports gradually became universally used as methods of identification, and finally as a way to establish that travel was a privilege, not a right. There are a few Americans who can't travel and 200 million Russians, but it's wrong however many it involves. This was the talk in the hostel halls, and there was little argument. As far as the accusation that we were being exploited by the Chinese for their propaganda purposes was concerned, some felt that they were instead exploiting the Chinese, in getting a free trip to an exciting place. Obviously the trip would cost a great deal, and China wanted a return. Whatever their motives, we were curious and interested enough either to use them or be used by them, depending on individual positions.

I spent the last few days frantically trying to find someone to help me to come back to Moscow, with little success except a tentative offer of a job editing English translations, and a trial manuscript to work on. Then we were off across Siberia.

The train ride was an adventure in itself. Simply riding, riding, incessant, forever, with that Walter Mitty ta-pocketa-pocketa-*pocketa-pocketa* noise the whole time. Nothing to do at all—but I luckily had the manuscript, some Tolstoy short stories, to edit. The rest of the crew didn't fare so well. Almost everyone was sick, but the few able-bodied divided their time between deciding, not very amicably, who should have his turn to read one of the five books on China that we had with us, playing poker with leftover roubles (the winner getting off at the next stop to buy vodka, and so on, until there wasn't any money left to gamble with), arguing with the two Russian interpreters we had along, arguing with each other, and playing that charming game, Who's the Spy? It became slightly obsessional, that naturally there was at least one State Department or FBI or whatever-it-is plant, who would be just the same as everybody else or more so, not to arouse suspicion. After this was first suggested, everyone started looking at everyone else most peculiarly. There was nothing for it but to get to know one another, and the conditions weren't exactly ideal. Neither were the results. But in the end the only thing of value was the ten-day-long travelogue outside the window.

It was wonderful. We found we seemed to have several layers of consciousness, and often, with no provocation, we fell through to the one below the last and suddenly *realized* where we were and what this was. Siberia! Somehow I had thought that it would all be cold and black and bleak, but found out soon how wrong that was. Why cold, even in the summer? It was warm, green and blue and white. It was vast, giving one the same sensation as trying to imagine how big is outer space. And many parts of it were indescribably beautiful, always changing violently. Past Kirov, Perm (Molotov): eruptions of hills, small farms, trees, fields; Sverdlovsk: steppe, boundless flatness; Omsk, Novosibirsk, the capital of Siberia: forests again, pine and white birch; Krasnoyarsk and Irkutsk, and the huge Lake Baikal; Ulan-Ude, Chita, and Mongol faces. We stopped briefly in many towns, and were met by brass bands, smiling Siberians, flowers. During the intervals people in the group got out and tore around, racing breathlessly back to catch the train again, although it always waited for them. Then on again, past tiny villages, closer to my original expectations, where the houses were primitive brown cabins, the ground brown mud, and even the people nearly brown, looking bent and spiritless under their load of hard living and boredom. Yet they had such natural hope around them, such earth, such resources—new, rich, uncultivated.

In China it was different. The land itself, after we had crossed the border, seemed used up and dead—but the people had shine and cheer. We rode for hours one evening through something that looked like an H. G. Wells futuristic wasteland: absolute flatness and nothingness and a setting sun, no sign of any kind of life, but now and then the hollow shells of old settlements. A very old crumbling roofless house silhouetted against a burnt-out sky. But the people—though they were surrounded by nothing but craggy eroded mountains or treeless swamp, and living in poverty beyond my wildest imagination in mud grass-covered huts—still achieved a brightness, if only through the introduction of one red gateway or the colour on a clothesline. And they *shone*, they walked with spirit and with their heads up, springily.

We missed connections at the boundary, so had to wait twenty-four hours in the station of a tiny Mongolian town, Manchouli. It was a worthwhile decompression chamber. Although no one was prepared for our being there, the local youth held an impromptu dance in the hotel, which appeared to be the only building of modern construction there. The others were pathetic, but still cheerful. Gaily painted signs hung outside small craft shops, and almost everyone had at least one caged bird hopping about outside his front door. There were *thousands* of children, some carrying others on their backs, running and playing everywhere, following us and laughing. And the 'newspaper'—a big blackboard on the path by the road covered with chalked characters. Women singing and washing clothes in the river. Nowhere the heaviness and intensity that is the traditional Russia. I felt as though I was breathing life again—here was light and movement.

There is too much to say about China which I couldn't say well enough, and this book is about Moscow. It was as exciting in reality as any dream. There is the remoteness, the 'oriental mystery' that always appeals to Westerners, but that seemed trivial in the face of seeing the new land, unlike any seen before, pioneering in a vast experiment.

I remember many things vividly. The multitudes of children everywhere, little ones with slit pants, running, squealing, laughing. They made it seem indisputable that every third child in the world *must* be Chinese. Peking, the Imperial Palace, pagodas and incredible age. The mountains were all lavender and jagged, and at last I understood why Chinese artists painted such weird mountains. Sometimes the scenery looked entirely like a Chinese painting. I hadn't thought it could. Receptions with leaders and a conference with prime minister Chou En-lai: brilliantly diplomatic, impressively strong and friendly. A two-day boat ride down the Yangtse. The children's palace in Shanghai, a millionaire's gorgeous mansion converted into paradise. The man in charge of re-educating the Shanghai prostitutes (Shanghai is cleaned up, of prostitutes, beggars, and opium dens). Buddhas. New buildings going up everywhere, constructed almost entirely by hand labour, and surrounded by scaffolding of bamboo and string. Chinese traditional medicine—acupuncture, the 3,000-year-old treatment of long needles manipulated in the body's nerve centres. It often works, curing a range of diseases, but no one quite knows why. The shops, with bright and well-designed merchandise, a plentiful supply of consumer goods compared to Russia. The bazaar in Peking. Curios, beautiful jade, scrolls. The poverty of the streets—and the smell. The people—delicacy, diplomacy, kindness, warmth. Exquisite food. Sour plum juice sold in old Coca-Cola bottles in street stalls. The Soviet embassy in Peking, where I went periodically to see about a re-entry permit. Solid and serious and heavy again —'It's impossible.' 'I must ask Moscow.' 'I have not heard from Moscow.' 'It is impossible.' The friends who took me boating at midnight on Pei Hai Lake in Peking. The parade on October 1st, National Day, when a half million people proved, if nothing else, how much they worshipped Mao. Canton.

We arrived in Canton simultaneously with the monsoon season: wind, dark grey sky, pouring rain, heat.

Its streets are individual in one way—each shop has its second floor projecting out above the street for protection from the rain and sun, supported by gaily coloured pillars. The climate is subtropical, and this was evident from wonderful fruit sold on the pavement by barefoot vendors who squatted beside it: red persimmons and a green star-shaped fruit with a name no one could translate for me. Palm trees, insects, heat.

Everywhere multitudes of children ran barefoot in the rain. There were more with no shoes than in the north, many wearing wooden clogs instead of cloth slippers. Mothers always had their babies with them, papoose-like on their backs in an intricately tied sling; and men wore straw tent raincoats. These things made Canton different.

But basically it was like all the Chinese cities I saw. The mud streets were small and the shack homes leaned precariously on one another, with the last shack in some rows leaning on a beautiful new apartment house or cultural palace. The shops were like caves, gaping holes in the wall. In a row, one selling ivory toothbrushes, then a pharmacy with curious powders and pills, even antlers, and a huge birth control display outside, then pens and long bamboo brushes, then baskets, clocks, clothing, shoes, books, a photography studio with one picture of Mao Tse-tung and one of Red Skelton in the window; at the end a little café with the customers sitting on tiny stools drinking tea and eating a kind of mess that simmered in a huge pot in a corner. Everything was shiningly clean.

We took a boat ride to see a sampan village, the biggest one in China. Our motor boat wove down the Pearl River in the pouring rain between junks, rafts and barges being poled or sculled and having the added obstacle of our wake to overcome. We passed Sha Mien island where the English and French once lived. 'No Chinese Allowed' was the law then; now the mansions were converted into government buildings or flats, and a mass of Chinese children played in the one-time sedate English country gardens. Where once an electrified fence on the shore enforced the law, the sampans were now tied up. The small boats were huddled in thousands close together like stepping stones across the brownish water. They were each about twenty feet long and five feet wide, only the middle section roofed in (with a conglomeration of tin scraps, rags and straw matting) and the undersides where they tipped up at the ends showing crazy patterns from decades of repairs.

The downpour had lessened by the time we reached the village, and people emerged on to the ends of their boats to stare at the 'high-noses.' We found out that there were 60,000 living there, and that until 1949 they had not been permitted to marry people from the shore, so not only had most of them lived on the boats all their lives, but all their ancestors had too. It had been an ingrown community of outcasts, its members barred from trade, school, forced to walk barefoot through the Canton streets, and despised by everyone on land.

Conditions had improved a great deal for them since the revolution, although they still lived far worse than most. But poverty was never real to me before and giving it a relativity seems ridiculous.

Now the river boat inhabitants had running water stations on each bank and no longer had to drink the water into which they threw everything. Clinics had been set up for mothers, and the infant mortality rate had been lowered from about 50 per cent pre-1949 to 3.6 per cent. Eighty per cent of the children were going to schools (on the English island), and their parents had jobs on shore instead of the fishing, ferrying and roaming to which they were once limited. Adult-education classes, infirmaries, and consumer co-operatives had been set up. Most important, the government was moving them all to the land as quickly as possible.

We were invited to visit some of the boats. I went into an average-looking one and met Ling Yu, a woman of about thirty, her small daughter and baby, and her brother. Like many of the Cantonese I saw, they were beautiful, racially mixed, with faces almost like Gauguin's Tahitians. They were barefoot and dressed in faded blue trousers and print shirts, and the little girl had a piece of wood tied to her behind to buoy her up if she fell into the water.

Ling Yu's boat was lined with polished boards, with a small storage space in the bow, a stove aft, and shelves under the roof with a couple of dishes on them. If she had anything else it was under the boards. With all this bareness, the surprising thing was that one of the walls was covered with expensively framed photographs and documents. She smiled proudly when I noticed them—her husband, she said, was a model worker in a paper mill and these were his awards. Model workers have more prestige than anyone in China; they achieve their titles by faster or improved methods of work.

She told us that she had lived on the same boat all her life, together with, at different times, from three to eight members of her family. Her father, now a factory worker and living on the shore, had been a ferryman and their days had been spent carrying people and goods, in their home, across the Pearl. Now, although things were much better for her, with half the family on shore and most of them working, she looked forward to nothing so much as leaving the boat altogether and for ever.

I had come there with sentimental memories of a children's book about a duck named Ping who lived on a sampan in China. When I was five this had seemed the ultimate in life. Now, after seeing it only briefly, I understood what Ling Yu meant.

Six weeks went by, full of days like that one. We moved from the industrial north-east to the more agricultural south and back again, stopping in the bigger cities and listening to people tell us of their changed lives. Nothing was hidden from us as far as I could tell; we were permitted to arrange our own itinerary, walk alone wherever and meet whomever we wanted. Everyone bent over backwards to see that no request was refused. At the same time they insisted on showing us the chief objects of their pride: factories, farms, public institutions, new buildings, and many things that weren't particularly novel to us but to the Chinese meant everything. Each of these things, each new truck, each brick, each inch upwards, represented to them a victory over their past of near-feudalism and poverty.

We found the official optimism absurdly unbelievable until it became obvious that everyone felt optimism. We were surrounded by millions of people whose every energy, ambition, dream, was, it seemed to me, completely involved not only with small things but with pulling their country up on its feet and finding a place in the world. That was the one, the only, important thing for any of the people I met, and it was catching. There was no choice but to think about it as seriously as they did. And so, click—there I was plunged straight into the confusion I had spent years carefully avoiding: the world's problems.

China's problems were provocative enough to begin on!

China gave me many new ideas about the concept of freedom. Like many others who have lived in a society which values freedom above everything, I considered it an absolute, and was appalled and indignant at any suggestion that it might be limited, whatever the circumstances. I carried this idea with me and never considered attaching any reservations to it until I began to have some comprehension of what I was seeing. I met capitalists and many who had lost much, who still had the same enthusiasm as those who had only gained. Everywhere I met agreement. Some agreed originally because they had no choice, and later sincerely, as a result of persuasion and explanation. That they really honestly did believe didn't much affect the fact that they were not free to disagree, and it still angered me. But eventually, after I realized that the whole situation could only be thought of in the most basic terms of *a bowl of rice a day*, I felt that perhaps it might be worth the price. The very unanimity of the people was the reason for the speed and the progress. The progress, first of all, fed people. Before, many were starving and homeless, and now they had enough to eat and a place to live. Which is more important, starving to death or limited freedom? It seemed to me that freedom doesn't mean very much in that context—it's almost a luxury. What will follow is something else, but the Chinese themselves had faith in the future. As one girl explained to me, 'There are no divergent interests; there is only one. We must build our society. We have no time to waste on choices. Now we must work, and avoid mistakes, and build up social consciousness in our people at the same time. Discipline is necessary until people think on a higher level. When the feeling of the collective is there, self-discipline is also. Then there will be collective discipline.'

I have no way of knowing whether her prophecy will come true, or how much would have to be surmounted first. In everything with which I came in contact, though, I found the Chinese extremely honest with themselves. I noticed that unlike some people, official and otherwise, in the Soviet Union, the Chinese criticized themselves and their mistakes frequently and loudly, and constantly asked for advice and criticism from others. Whether this is something basically Chinese, or comes from the fact that the revolution is so recent that people remember clearly what they are fighting, or is the result of wise leadership, I can't tell.

All the people, from the leaders down, are subject to this criticism. The rectification campaign, in full swing while we were there, served as the force behind re-examination of everything. One aspect of this is what they call 're-education'—those who dissent are persuaded to agree. Those with 'wrong ideas' are censured and converted, and end up with self-criticizing with deep humility, determined to remould themselves in the pattern of society. I could never completely understand this mechanism because I've never known people made that way, but more and more I saw the value of it in a place like China. If it works, it means that the society can move forward literally single-mindedly, with no detours, no useless violent purges (which were discarded in favour of re-education), and with each member utterly convinced, working happily, productively, and living fully up to his potential.

'It is inevitable; China will get better steadily, and there are no limits. And it is simply the spirit of 650 million people that will do it.' One man said that to me, but I felt that any of the 650 million might have, and no one needed to anyway because it was everywhere and obvious. This spirit was crackling, energetic, soaring. It is created most of all by the feeling of importance and dignity invested in each individual—he *matters* now. Before he was a second-class human being, both in the world and in his own country. Machine-gun nests outside the foreign colonies, or signs reading 'Dogs and Chinese not admitted', reminded him of it all over his own cities. Not only does he now have a status in his country's eyes, but in the eyes of the world. Nationalism is something entirely new to him, and its power is stronger because of it. He knows he owes his status to his country's rise, so he works for his country, for the people, not solely for personal gain. I have never seen such unselfishness on a mass scale before, or such hard work, or such a desire for self-improvement for the common good. But in China, every person I saw had that light in his eyes.

The more I saw the more I wanted to see, and the more I thought that China's experiment could work. Power is frightening, and power can be abused by anyone who has too much of it. The adulation heaped on Mao Tse-tung was incredible. Also I felt that the excesses of the anti-rightist campaign were in danger of destroying much of the good that followed Chairman Mao's 'Let a hundred flowers bloom' speech. But for the time being there appeared to be many causes for hope. First, the leaders seemed honest, and they had a good chance of remaining that way because they did not lose contact with the people they served, as most leaders seem to do in most places. Party discipline required them to do physical labour one day a week with the workers. They worked intensely hard almost all the time at their own jobs besides, and received few privileges except prestige. They were no new class. Second, they were as open to criticism as everyone else. Most important, they really listened to criticism, they wanted it, accepted it with humility, and had a tremendous willingness to learn.

Maybe I and all the others were, as the State Department put it, 'communist tools'. If we were brainwashed I didn't feel a thing; this is what I saw, after going there in a state of comprehensive ignorance. I don't expect to sell anything to anyone, but I think it would be a very good thing if others went too; even if they were to see something entirely different, they might all understand each other better.

2

Sputniks and Old Lace

THE CHINA TRIP was over, and those of us who were still left in Peking got up before dawn one day to catch the jet to Moscow. Almost all the foreigners who had come for the big October 1st celebrations had gone, and Peking was taking down its decorations and red banners as we drove to the airport. Crowds of people were there to see off Kadar, the Hungarian party secretary, who was travelling with us, and the last Chinese face I saw as the roaring began was that of Chou En-lai.

Everyone was in a state of excitement, some because of the jet-ride, some worrying about who would meet us with what from the American embassy, and the amateur journalists in the group concentrating on cornering Kadar for an interview. He was surrounded by 'assistants' and 'secretaries' (they said) who, strangely, could have doubled for heavyweight wrestlers. But they got an interview, and everyone got his autograph. Some had him sign American delegation souvenir cards left over from the festival, right below the picture of the American flag.

The plane was a superb contrast: Victorian decorations at nine miles a minute. After the ten-day eternity of the trans-Siberian train ride, it was altogether a fantastic experience in time. We screamed up into the clear air and before long the earth looked like a papier maché contour map. The worn

19

brown mountains of China looked too tired to care about the
new experiment of the men who owned them. But in fact
there was no evidence of the experiment out here, far from
any city. Before we got too high, we could still see the poverty
of the shacks below—people living as they probably had for a
thousand years, while the silver future passed over their heads.

Soon we flew over Lake Baikal, and down below by its side
we could see a tiny dot of smoke puffing from a train like the
one we had gone in. We crossed the lake in five minutes; the
train would take half a day. Then Irkutsk, and Russia again.
In two and a half hours we were three days from Peking! The
houses were wood again, the people Western again, and the
airport buffet was all lace, crystal and garnet-coloured plush,
and full of solid Soviet types stoking up on eats and drinks
with determined concentration. Suddenly we all felt as heavy
as they looked.

Ten hours after leaving Peking we plummetted through the
clouds into Moscow airport. In the waiting room a man from
our embassy introduced himself, and suddenly the place was
still with tension. He asked to see our passports but no one
moved; then he went to each one in turn. Some gave them
to him, but he returned them right away and checked off
things on a list. Then he told us to go to the first embassy
we came to outside the Communist bloc and give them our
passports. He wouldn't answer questions.

The airport was thrown into utter chaos by our arrival. No
Russians were there to meet us, no one knew where we were
to go, no one cared, and no one spoke English. It had taken
eight hours' flying time to go 4,000 miles, but it took another
six to travel the few feet out the airport door. Solid women
sat behind desks clicking their abacuses and viewing us with
complete indifference. Planes arrived and left, the faces in the
waiting room changed, and finally a frantic young man showed
up to deal with this problem. He made a great deal of noise
and a lot of phone calls, but couldn't find anyone in town
willing to be responsible for us, and that was an unprecedented
situation. It would have been unbearable anywhere else, but

the Russians can be so charming about their inefficiency that it seemed like a mad comedy. In the end, no nearer a solution but with a good day's work behind him, he packed us off to the airport hotel for the night.

Although I was discouraged by this performance, I thought the next morning that I'd have one last fling at staying, anyway. Foreigners just aren't allowed to stay and live in the Soviet Union, I kept hearing, and finally I believed it. But there was nothing to lose. And suddenly miracles started happening. Within four hours, with not a trace of red tape or any other difficulty, I met three people who said yes. YES! Just like that! Oh what a word that is in Russia.

Later I found that there was a sort of circular gimmick involved. One needed three things, without one of which the other two were impossible. The first was a job, then a place to live, then a sponsoring organization. A sponsoring organization says that it's out of the question because you have no job. If you find a job they say no good we have nowhere for you to live. If someone is willing to put you up, you can't get a permit from the police to reside in Moscow without a sponsoring organization. It's really foolproof. Just somehow I managed to get two yeses: the job I had tried for came through, and an invitation to stay with an English journalist and his family. The third yes wasn't difficult after that.

Remnants of the delegation to China continued to turn up and filter through Moscow bound for points west, but I soon got established in a sort of routine and both China and Americans seemed a long way off. My work, editing English translations of Russian classics for the Foreign Languages Publishing House, was extremely well paid (up to five roubles per page, and a page rarely took more than three minutes), as are all artistic professions. Because there wasn't enough space at the publishing office I worked at home, and could live adequately on one or two hours of it a day. There seemed little point in doing more, as the extra roubles wouldn't have represented very much, and I wanted to use the time seeing what Moscow was all about.

The city felt very cold and lonely after the festival. It had seemed so cheerful and beautiful then, because the flags and pictures and decorations, and the summer green, gave it the colour it now lacked. The people, too, weren't the same. The electric gaiety and excitement had faded, the crowds in Manege Square had gone, and no one gathered around me in the streets anymore. Everyone seemed so quiet and grave. That was how it felt at first, and still might to anyone new. But gradually I began to meet the Russians, and after I got to know something about them I never noticed those things again. Maybe they had never existed in the first place, or maybe they didn't seem important anymore.

I was walking down Gorky Street one day, feeling very lonely and not understanding anything. Preoccupied people jostled me on the sidewalk, and I felt no sympathy for any of them, mainly because they felt none for me. I wanted to buy some oranges but the shops were so full and everyone in such a hurry that I didn't think they'd have any patience with my phrase-book Russian.

A boy stopped me suddenly and asked me an incomprehensible question; everyone was always asking me for directions and making involved speeches at me as if I knew what I was doing. This time he didn't even wait for my 'I don't understand Russian', but said in English, 'You're American? I thought you were, from your shoes'. He walked along with me, gesticulating and stumbling out his English. 'I never have met an American before, I was in Siberia this summer and was not here for the festival. Would you help me with my English? I would like very much to know an American! My name is Sergei. Why are you here?' He stopped for breath, or perhaps he'd exhausted his supply of English, but in the gap I asked him if he would help me buy some oranges.

'Of course!' he said, and ploughed through the nearest mobs of Muscovites in a professional way to a fruit and vege- table store. We went to the right counter and I saw a stout flustered woman shovelling oranges into paper cones from a huge crate, while scores of shoppers shouted questions and waved bits of paper at her. Taking no notice of the others, Sergei joined the uproar and asked her the price of the oranges, then steered me back through the crowd to the cashier. We joined the end of the queue and he continued his stream of words.

'Are you a journalist? My brother is a journalist, now he is in Paris. I spoke to him on the telephone two days ago! I would like to be a journalist, I would love to see Paris, but it is probably impossible in my work. Oh well, maybe yes, maybe no, maybe rain, maybe snow. I am in the engineering institute.'

I told him I wasn't a journalist, that I worked in Moscow for a publishing house. Apparently 'publishing house' is a euphemism for brothel in Russian, or something like that, anyway I always got rather strange reactions. Nobody would ever tell me why. Sergei asked me all about it and eventually figured out that I was living in Moscow, and was terribly pleased. 'Oh, then we will see each other. I have very many interesting friends, they will like very much to meet you.'

The woman behind us shouted at him to get on with it, he was at the head of the line; so he bought a ticket from the cashier, with her inevitable abacus, and we returned to the fruit counter. The conversation lagged temporarily while he joined the paper wavers, but he was big and had a loud voice, so we didn't have to wait long. I thanked him for his help. Even at the end of my stay I didn't always have the courage to do much shopping.

Out in the street again he continued to talk agitatedly, then arranged to take me to meet his mother the next evening. This was indeed an honour: all boys in Russia with serious intentions are supposed to introduce their girls to their parents and homes to get things started.

He met me at the Bolshoi Theatre the next evening and brought me to his home in a taxi. His family's apartment surprised me; it was large and well furnished. It registered then how comparatively well-dressed Sergei was, in a Western-cut sports jacket and beige suede shoes. His mother was the same; she was thinner than most Russian women of her age and there was a touch of chic about her dress. She was very glad to see me, and sat with us and smiled whenever we did, though she didn't understand what we said.

Sergei immediately, terribly, intensely, wanted to know all about jazz, and was simply horror-struck to find that I, a real American girl, didn't know anything. He switched on a tape recorder and I recognized some of the latest American hit parade music, as well as old songs and the newest jazz, but they are all lumped together under the general heading of 'jezz'.

'I got them from the Voice of America,' he explained. 'Also some of my friends have records from the festival.'

I asked him about the festival and how it had affected his friends. He had been in Siberia, he said again, working as a member of a Komsomol farming team—he had been in trouble last year and had to redeem himself. One of the worst *tragedies* of his life had been missing the festival. His friends had met many interesting people and had bought foreign clothes. Smoothing his suit, he said he had had to buy it fourth hand from one of his 'beezness' friends who got it from someone else who got it from an Italian boy. The price had gone up almost geometrically with each sale. The first person to buy it had been thrown out of Komsomol (Young Communist League) for standing outside the hostels every night for a week to buy things.

A maid, one of two, called us into the dining room to have tea. It was the only apartment I ever saw with a dining room. 'Tea' turned out to be cold meat, cheese, fruit, three kinds of bread, three kinds of cake, jam, caviar, and tea. No one ate very much, but his mother looked tragic at any refusal of mine, and I couldn't go without attempting one of everything.

The next time I saw Sergei, he took me to the restaurant at the Sovietskaya Hotel. It is a huge marble room about three storeys high, full of chandeliers and gilt. Echoing through its vastness came music from a determined-looking band on a stage at one end, accompanying a throaty soprano who stood about half an inch away from the microphone warbling a Russian translation of St. Louis Woman. All Sergei's jet-set friends were there, watching with envy as he escorted his Real American Girl through the door. He had obviously brought off the *coup* of the year.

We sat at a table on the side, Sergei glancing now and then at his friends to see if they were watching us. They were. They were a group of about ten, the boys in foreign suits, often the wrong size, looking a sort of combination of Elvis Presley and James Dean; and the girls heavily and badly made-up and wearing simple suits and dresses. The hair was the most unusual note: the girls wore neither the long braids or buns up behind nor the frizzy permanents I saw everywhere else—an improvement—but some of the boys had managed an English teddy boy type of thing.

They danced a lot, drank a lot, and kept on looking. I think it was even more than Sergei had anticipated, and to keep things rolling he went over and invited them for the next week to a party for me.

Sergei and his friends were *stiliagi*—style-chasers—and in many ways he was typical. Some weeks later I found out his whole story. His father, who had died in the war, had been a general, and Sergei had been brought up with all the money he wanted and nothing to buy with it. The family had had a big black Zim to drive around in and a chauffeur to drive it, two maids and a cook and his father's assistant, a *dacha* in the country, and English, French and piano tutors for Sergei and his brother. The brother had made good as a journalist, but Sergei's life was a constant search for something exciting. He wasn't very interested in his career, though he had confidence that he'd be a success because of influential friends. Every evening was spent living it up in a restaurant or at a party dancing rock 'n' roll. He never read anything, but used up a lot of time speculating over foreign things. Nothing was any good unless it was foreign, he thought. Often he or those like him gave me foreign pens, jewellery, cigarette cases or holders, lighters, sometimes even American cigarettes and chewing gum, or anything else they could get from the beez-nessmen around (who existed nicely but precariously on rake-offs from transactions in foreign merchandise) because that was the prize. Yet actually material things meant very little to him; they were just a way to buy something else, which in turn was meaningless. In fact, nothing really mattered. 'I want exciting,' he put it—that was his only ambition.

To get 'exciting' he had organized a sort of revolutionary game once, with many other boys all over the city. Inspired by reports that filtered through about Hungary (one of them even had the copy of *Life* with the pictures of the revolution), they planned a demonstration, but one of the boys turned out to be a 'pirate' (informer) and some of them were arrested. Sergei got out of it after a short spell in the Lubyanka, presumably through the same friends who would later help him with his career, and immediately afterwards he volunteered to fight the British, French and Israeli aggressors at Suez, but wasn't taken up on it.

He was still very young, in his last year at the engineering institute and basically extremely intelligent, but was bitter and disillusioned about everything in life.

'It's a *black* life,' he would say morbidly. There was nothing that interested him. I told him once that I knew young people everywhere who felt that too, but he just shrugged and altered it to 'black life, special for Russians', yet with no specific criticism that applied to his depressed condition.

Sergei had hopelessly bourgeois values, with no means of fulfilling them.

Through the efficient Moscow grapevine, David, a man I had met during the Youth Festival, heard I was back and somehow tracked me down. The next week, as I was finishing dressing to go out to Sergei's party, the doorbell rang and David appeared. All I could see of him, all I could ever see of him, was a huge grin radiating leathery creases all over his face.

He sat down and looked over the room, then got up and

peered in the back of the radio. Seeing nothing to worry him, he looked around again, spotted a hole high up in the wall, adjusted a chair under it and poked about with the end of a pencil. Finally, appearing satisfied, he sat down again. This extraordinary performance, he explained, was to find the microphone.

'Nu, just to be safe,' he said, and turned up the radio to a deafening intensity.

David had come to the hostel where the American delegation was staying during the festival. Many of us were sitting around watching television, recovering from the Asian flu. One of the Americans, a bearded artist from Brooklyn, was sketching in a corner, and the minute David walked in the artist was fascinated by his grin-wrinkles and asked him to pose. He was a little, sort of middle-aged man, wearing the sagging and shoddy clothes of a worker and totally unlike all the others I'd met. I went over to see him and the sketch and David said 'Hello, I am David', in a very deep bass voice that didn't sound as though it could possibly belong to him. He immediately started telling me about himself, with hardly a pause, almost as if he were dictating a short autobiography. He spoke in a strange ponderous English, pronouncing each word distinctly and repeating every other one. His vocabulary was almost Dickensian. He said he had taught himself English in the last eight years by reading simplified English classics and keeping notes of the words he didn't know. He had a friend who had taught him how to pronounce the words, but he had never spoken in English before the festival.

I asked him a few questions which started him off, and soon he was ignoring all the noise and scuffling in the room, and the annoyed artist, who kept nagging him to keep still.

'I am a Jew,' he began. 'I am thirty-eight, and I work in an automobile factory.' He used to work in another factory, until he got into trouble. He had written a satirical poem about his 'chief' and in the end had got fired. I asked him about it and he did not hesitate to give all the details. He had been a trade union leader in his factory, and in this position tried to improve conditions. For one thing, he said, his chief had made them work from 8 o'clock till 2 on Saturdays without a break, and he had tried to do something about that. But the chief was a bureaucrat and didn't care about the workers, only about fulfilling the Plan and getting personal glory. 'And he was anti-Leninist,' David gravely intoned this serious, most final criticism.

One Saturday afternoon David had arranged for the workers to go to the place where Lenin died, and had obtained the use of the factory bus. But when they had finished work and went outside to board the bus, it was gone and they were told that the chief had taken it for his own use, leaving the message that they could use a small car instead.

David was really worked up about this. He gesticulated in his rage and the artist was getting angrier and angrier. 'The car wasn't *big* enough!' David said, 'and he *knew* it. So I became very furious and I wrote that poem about him. I didn't say it was he but everyone knew, and I lost my job. Then I lost my flat, of course, because I got it through the factory. And my wife left me, she wouldn't stay with me without food or flat, and I don't know where she went.'

He had taken the matter to court, he went on, and had fought the case for six months. Nobody would help him and 'they' kept it going on and on, because they knew he had no food and nowhere to live. Finally he had to give it up because otherwise he would have starved, so he never had been able to prove he was right, and that was what made him so furious. Besides the principle involved, he didn't mind too much about the rest. It had shown that his wife wasn't worth anything, and he hadn't liked that job so much anyway. He had found this other one in the automobile factory and things weren't so bad. He grinned again.

Another American came over then and David introduced himself again, saying 'I'm David, I'm a Jew. Are you a Jew?' The boy answered yes, he was, and asked David if he spoke Yiddish. For the first time David looked hesitant. He glanced round to see if anyone else was listening, then said quietly,

'Yes. And I am very interested in Israel. Have you ever been to Israel?' They spoke in Yiddish for a while, then David said he had to go. He lived in the outside rim of Moscow and had to catch the last train. As a matter of fact . . . he grinned and then simply shook with glee. 'Ah, I don't have enough words to explain . . .' he said sadly after his laughter had subsided. He searched through a very large briefcase for a dictionary, leafed through its pages, then with acute surprise exclaimed: 'There *isn't* one for this! Well! Hm! You see, we have to have a *propiska* to live in Moscow; this is the best place and every-one wants to live here. I suppose you do not know what this *propiska* is? It is a stamp in the passport with the address, and without it no one can stay here, you must go to another place or something. And I do not have it, because of that trouble I was in, and "they" do not know!' He laughed again.

'*Nu*, I must go. Will you write to me when you are back in Moscow?' He wrote his address in my book, and under-neath in big crude black letters, put 'DAVID, I AM BEST SOVIET FRIEND! ! ! ! !' Then he said that we must not write to him from abroad, and that when we came back we must mail letters from a post office, not a hotel (because all foreigners stay at hotels), and have the envelope addressed by a Russian.

He looked across the room to where a couple was laughing and fooling around. A girl jumped up and a boy caught her in his arms and whirled her about. 'Ah, you people,' David said gently, his grin fading. 'You are human, you people.' He left.

Now he was with me again and very angry that I hadn't written to him the minute I arrived. I apologized and asked him what had happened to him. He still held his job in the automobile factory, he said, and no one had found out yet that he didn't have a *propiska*, so everything in life was won-derful. Grin. 'And I have practised English for you,' he said. 'I have a story to tell you,' and he pulled out of his briefcase an English-Russian dictionary, a Russian-English dictionary, and a thick, tattered notebook full of words, all of which he kept referring to as he struggled through the story.

'There were some men in . . . mm . . . *heaven*,' he found the word triumphantly. 'They wanted to make a Communist . . . group, and they must choose a leader. All of them wanted to be the leader. They all talked at once. They were very . . .' he looked in the notebook '. . . conceited. Only one very old bearded man simply sat in the corner, reading a newspaper, he didn't care. The others were fighting, but they couldn't decide, not even after many hours. Finally someone thought they should ask the old man, who was so modest, if he would like to be leader. "Why not you, old man?" someone asked him. "Oh, it's no use for me, it's quite impossible," he said to them. "Why so? You might be just what we need." "For two reasons, it is impossible," the man said. "First, I have many connections with foreigners. And two, I am a Jew."

'You know who it was?' David asked, too impatient to wait for the punch-line. 'Karl Marx!'

We talked for a while longer, then I asked him to come to the party with me. He hesitated and tried desperately to think of excuses, but eventually I coaxed him.

When we arrived things had already got under way—jazz, vodka, and lots of noise from the twenty-odd people there. They weren't all *stiliagi*; some were artists, some older, near David's age. David came into the room behind me, and suddenly there was a hush. I introduced him, but no one seemed at all inclined to talk to him, even after I explained to several of them apart that he was my friend and a very nice person. Eventually he was accepted by one group and joined in a discussion with them.

Sergei stood and listened to him for a few minutes, then called me aside and took me into another room. He shut the door behind him and looked around. 'He's a spy,' he said.

'Sergei, what a perfectly ridiculous thing to say!' It was funny. 'I've known David since the festival—he's absolutely straight and thinks the same as you do about a lot of things.'

'I don't care what you think. You don't know. It's our way of *life*. I can tell, I have an instinct. I can sense it immediately. Why did you bring him here anyway?'

'I thought you'd like him; I do. I'm sorry, but I just don't understand at all.'

'Come here, I want to show you something.' He led me into the dining room and pointed to a place in the ceiling. It was a piece of board covering an air vent, and painted over.

'My father did that when we first moved here. Look, here's another.' He showed me one in the hall. 'And the telephone.' He turned the phone upside down and tapped the bottom with his index finger. It was plastered with cardboard.

'What do you think my father did that for? He was *general*, very good Soviet. But he was afraid, and so am I, and so is everyone else. It's our way of *life*, Sally!' His anger gave way to sadness, or perplexity. 'You know, at the institute I have a group of about twenty friends. Four of them are pirates. We must be special friendly with them, though everyone knows. There's nothing we can do about it. That's about how it is everywhere—one from every five people is a pirate. And I've had enough experience to know one when I see one. Your spy friend David! It's our way of life, Sally,' he sighed and cracked his knuckles.

I argued with him and told him a little about David, but he had an answer for everything and the more he went on the more afraid I became. Perhaps David *was* a spy. What had I said to him? I desperately tried to remember every conversation we had had, and my anxiety increased as the evening dragged on. I didn't know what I was afraid of, it just wasn't logical, it made no *sense*. But the fear had been communicated and had done its job.

David and I left early; I couldn't stand it anymore. We walked back home through the first snowfall, but I was so preoccupied I hardly noticed. The streets were very quiet and gobs of white soon covered up the grey stone. Now and then a figure loomed up and passed by. I had the feeling I used to have as a child, that I was acting in a movie, but this time I felt disgusted because the script was so bad. I kept arguing with myself that rationally the whole thing was absolutely stupid, but it just didn't help. What could I *do?* I was terrified of saying another word to him.

'I must say something to you,' David broke the silence suddenly, and I felt myself stiffen. If he was going to ask me something, I'd watch myself, I thought. I tried to control my nerves and be ready to answer anything.

'That friend of yours—Sergei. I don't trust him. I can tell, we all can after what we've . . .'

He stopped, because I was laughing. He looked at me, horrified, and then I realized that it wasn't funny at all; it was grotesque. Didn't anyone trust anyone? Is everybody so afraid of something that isn't there? How is it ever possible to be normal and natural? What happens to human values in an atmosphere like that? What had just happened to me?

I told him all of it and then asked him some of these things. He said he would introduce me to some people who could tell me—they were young and their English was better.

'I don't care anymore, you see,' he stopped walking. 'A person gets used to it, or gets tired of worrying about it. I'm just tired. When I was younger, I liked to sit for hours and talk about freedom and art and politics. Now I've had enough talking. We talk about art but there *is* no art, we talk about freedom but there *is* no freedom. No one can do anything, there is never any . . . action. Only talk.'

We started walking again in silence, then he suddenly broke it.

'Why did you come here?' he was nearly sobbing. 'You are the first healthy person I have met. We are sick here.'

Suddenly I remembered a New Yorker, caught up in the competitive rat-race, saying nearly the same thing. An Englishman, concerned with the symptoms of decline, had too. None of us was very different.

Pro and Con

WHO WAS SICK, really? I kept meeting people who agreed with David and Sergei, but there were more who thought the opposite, who had deep faith in the Soviet system. Some of them were of little value to me—they fitted into a special category, the aggressively pro-Soviet. They felt compelled to push their beliefs strenuously at any opportunity, becoming defensive about things I hadn't even mentioned. They were for everything, everything was wonderful, and I can't believe anyone who is for everything. There was never any profit in talking to people like that because I could easily have read what they said, in the same words furthermore, in an official Soviet history. Unfortunately these are too often the type of Russian whom foreigners meet—they are so perfect, their beliefs fit in so neatly with the current line, that they are usually the ones who are exported officially or used as interpreters to foreign tourists. During the festival most of our interpreters were like that, presumably because the Americans were the logical people to deserve them most. They wore bell-bottomed trousers (Sergei once said that 'very good Soviet man always wears wide trousers—very important. Wider the trousers, more loyal the man') and hated jazz and smoked long-filtered Russian cigarettes (*papirosi*). They quoted Lenin, constantly and vociferously, to back up their statements (like the Bible, with its wealth of contradictions, it was possible to find support for almost anything), and they defended absolutely everything except those things which *Pravda* had recently criticized. They appeared to have lost the habit of thinking, if they ever had it.

I tried to be friendly with some of our interpreters at first when I was willing to latch on to anything at all that could teach me something about Russia. Once I cornered one of them during lunch, and asked him questions. He was overwhelmingly puritanical, and rigidly disapproved of my smoking and even of my wearing lipstick. His wife, whom he brought to meet us once, had neither vice. He wouldn't allow it in any case, he said. The two of them studied practically all the time when they weren't working, never drank ('it makes men like beasts') and never had anything to do with frivolous entertainment. He was a student of journalism but, he said, he was ashamed that he would never do physical work, only mental. He didn't believe in the superiority of the intellectual because that would create a stratified society, and one couldn't look down on the workers. He so obviously *did* look down on the workers. But 'in the Soviet Union, ever-r-ry-body can do ever-r-ry-thing'. He went on to say that he was very lucky to have been brought up so well that now he is intelligent and can be a journalist—naturally, intelligence is entirely due to environment. I tried to argue with him about that from what I could remember of my college psychology course, or even Lysenko, but he refused to even consider that this might not be entirely true. He was the same with any other subject that came up, sticking unbendingly to what he'd been taught and having not the slightest spirit of inquiry. His conception of the rest of the world seemed to be some weird universal Dickensian slum, where everyone was miserable, out of work, suffering from malnutrition, and sleeping on the streets. He conceded that perhaps some of us looked all right even if our fathers were capitalists, but beyond that he couldn't go. There wasn't much point in pursuing it anyway; I felt exhausted.

Our interpreter and those like him were the bright young

men whom the party values most, but whom I thought the country's biggest liabilities. They will always support and justify the status quo, they will become bureaucratic leaders who will never think or correct even the most obvious wrongs, and they will hate the West, blindly and passionately, because they are ignorant of it.

But there are so many others who have faith based on thought; they recognize and admit their country's faults, but have real belief in its basic good. If a better world is made there, it will be because of them, the constructive criticizers. One of them was Kolya, a young man who had a good job on a newspaper, a happy marriage and two healthy young children. I had met him during the festival too, when he had been constantly wandering around trying to find someone to interview. Later, when I came back, he often invited me to his home or asked me to join him and his wife and friends in nights out at the theatre or restaurants. None of the others spoke English, so I argued in a corner with Kolya.

He had seen the worst of things and didn't look at the situation blindly by any means. While his father had fought in the war, he and his mother had stayed in Leningrad during the blockade. His mother had starved to death by his side, and he had stayed by her body for two days until someone found him, nearly dead himself. The rest of the war he spent in a children's home where he at least had warmth and enough to eat, after many months of bare survival on a small piece of black bread a day, and no heat through a terrible winter.

When his father came back from the front they had moved to Moscow and he had gone to the university, married a student, and later got the job that he still held. During the worst years of the arrests one of the cars pulled up outside his own house one night and his father had been taken. He died in a Siberian camp. Subsequently Kolya's best friend and several acquaintances were also arrested. He knew as well as anyone that they were innocent and that it was a terrible injustice; those things still haunt him, but increase his determination that they are over and will never happen again. The future looks bright to him, and although he recognizes that there are mistakes, he is confident that his country is paving the way to a better life for mankind; and he will be among those who will work for this dream to come true.

I often confronted Kolya with some of the anti-Soviet remarks I had heard from others to get his reactions. He was upset that I had wasted time on hooligans and other worthless scum—'They are not typical, they are simply silly, they will give you wrong ideas.' Nevertheless he agreed with some of their criticism; artistic freedom worried him, as a writer, the most. Lack of freedom in general distressed him, but he felt that to a large extent it had been necessary and that, as the country grew materially and more people were educated, freedom would logically follow as a result of pressure from below.

'Education is the thing of main importance,' he said, 'but also the material life must be improved. In not too long a time, our standard of living will compare favourably with yours. When that happens, freedom to travel will come next. Soviet nationalism will not suffer then, and we won't have to worry about the dissatisfied. People will see another world, but will come back appreciating theirs.

'As you have seen, there are many people here who think in terms of flats and clothes and material luxuries, just as they would anywhere. Their unhappiness here is a result of a lack of these things, which they would lack in any case. Most of them don't understand how much worse things could have been for them, but for socialism. They're bitter and they complain, and many think that capitalism is better because people have more *things*. When there are more things, these petty people will be satisfied. It's not a question of freedom; they don't know what it is. If they could travel freely now, for instance, perhaps some wouldn't come back.'

I told him about the people I'd seen in China, who have far less than any Russian, yet are willing to sacrifice to the group even that which they have, because they believe in their country so fervently. It was like that here once, he answered.

But a revolutionary spirit doesn't last, although perhaps it had a chance in China. 'Here, the fight was soon over, and people wanted results. Many couldn't fit into the hardship that was necessary to achieve the results quickly. Who can blame them? The abuses were terrible. They want a good life. But they'll have it, you know, even though many don't believe it. Lots of them are just completely cynical and full of hate, and have no faith in anything.'

'Don't you think there's more to it than that?' I asked. 'Their attitudes count. The way they all talk about the sputniks—you know, I've met almost no one who cares at all about them. They think that at least some of the money spent on basic and futuristic industry should have gone into consumer goods, and to give them a better life. I met a woman the other day who said that it was fine about "them up there" (did she mean the sputniks or the leaders?) but why couldn't she buy a teapot. All she wants is a new teapot.'

'Well, of course—to some extent they're right, those people, but they don't understand the implications of our sputniks. This is a signal to the world that we're there, right next to them, and that soon we'll be ahead in teapots and everything else. It also shows that we want peace. Now that we're ahead of them, it would be ludicrous to wait until they catch up if we really want war. This just shows that we have it, we're not using it, we want peace. What could be more logical—but it's funny that so few believe us. I see their magazines and newspapers in my work, and it looks to me as if they are far more serious about war than they admit. All those diagrams and maps showing the new weapons, and "How We Could Destroy Russia in 6½ Minutes". We may have anti-American propaganda, but nothing as bloodthirsty as that.'

'What about Khrushchev?'

'Good man—shrewd, very clever. We were fooled at the beginning by his simplicity, but in fact he is just what we want, wise and a superb diplomat. He has a lot to overcome, but if anyone can do it, he can.'

'And Malenkov?'

'He was all right—he pacified the teapot people—but he made mistakes that could have hurt the people more in the long run. It was right that he should go, and the old clique too, Molotov and the others. They were wrong in the opposite way. But Nikita Sergeievich is moderate; he knows what he is doing, and he is strong—he does it well.

'The fact is—you know it and I know it—things are bad here now. Many things are terrible. But most of them are left from the hash the old man made of things. The main thing to remember is that five years ago things were far worse, and if you come again in five years from now you'll hardly recognize it. We really will beat America in butter, meat and milk, like they say. Then everything else. This country is growing, steadily and absolutely surely, despite any setbacks and mistakes. We're moving, and we're moving with history.

'Do you know what it means to someone, to live here and feel part of this progress?'

I felt very confused. I could understand Kolya and his faith, but it was just as easy to agree with someone on the other side. Sometimes I felt that it was all some mad ping-pong game, with me as the ball, being whacked back and forth from one end of the table to the other.

My bewilderment grew when I spoke to David's friends, the ones he wanted me to meet to explain their ideas to me. I had many talks with one of them, Shura, a very brilliant and intense student, who looked like my vision of Raskolnikov. He lived with his mother, grandmother, and brother Yuri, in a typical Moscow room of fifteen square metres which had been made into three rooms by using wardrobes and cupboards as partitions. They shared a kitchen and bathroom with ten families.

The first time we went there David warned me to look as Russian as possible, because to get to Shura's room we had to pass through the communal kitchen, where five or eight women stood around and gossiped and showed huge interest in anyone who came through. Naturally, Shura explained, at least one of these women worked for the secret police ('there's one in every flat') and he would get into trouble for seeing foreigners.

In the main section of the room hung the inevitable fringed lamp, orange, over a round table, around which we sat for nightlong discussions while his grandmother produced endless cups of tea and laid out every kind of snack they could afford.

Shura's English was about twice as good as mine. His vocabulary was vast. He began right away to tell me about his history and ideas; apparently he was satisfied that I was reliable, although one of the things that came out in our first discussion was that his father had once told him: 'Anyone starting a counter-revolutionary conversation with a stranger is either a fool or a stool.' Shura's father had been the son of a Polish immigrant falsely accused of collaborating with the Germans during the war, as was practically everyone, Shura said, who had even remote connections w ith foreigners. Fifteen million people had suffered for that, he said. His father had died in an arctic concentration camp; he was an intellectual and weak and couldn't survive the cold and the insufficient food. It was an interesting comparison between Shura and Kolya: they had this experience in common but had developed from it in diametrically opposite directions.

We started talking about the festival. He said that in the months before, Moscow, 'although it is already the only civilized place in the USSR', had been given a face-lifting: new paint and plaster, and fences to hide the worst eyesores. The shops had been stocked with new clothes, and anti-Western propaganda had been stepped up. The effect the festival had on the people was very great, he said; it had been one more thing in a long series lately to increase discontent. He believed that the government regretted holding it at all, because it had been living proof to the Russians that people from the capitalist countries not only were not oppressed but in fact were happy and lively in a way no Russians were, and were materially far better off. Also, many Russians were now writing to foreigners all over the world, and the government had no control over coded letters or anything that might be

going back and forth. 'They must be getting quite an un-
wieldy filing system. Naturally all foreign mail is opened and
photographed. It's not read immediately, just filed away in
that person's record until he gets in trouble.'

Many Muscovites during the festival had stopped behaving
with their usual caution, he went on. He said he had heard
that many Russian girls, he thought about eighty, had become
far too friendly with foreigners and that they had been
systematically rounded up during and after the festival; their
heads were shaved, and they were sent to the virgin lands.

But such things were rarer than before, he said—and seemed
strangely sorry to be able to say it. For one thing the caution
—no one talks to anyone they don't know. For another 'there
aren't many people left to be arrested—anyone with a spark
of imagination and/or courage was already taken care of. But
the people are getting tired of feeling afraid, and won't put
up with as much as they once would. For instance when
Molotov was discredited, many workers asked to hear *his*
side of the story. They didn't get it, of course, but they never
would have even *asked* before. Under Stalin they would take
almost anything. He was the father figure; the people needed
a god, particularly for the war. It's quite true that many
soldiers died with Stalin's name on their lips. The things he
was responsible for—they were inevitable, I think. If not
Stalin then someone else. Even if Lenin had lived it would
have been the same. He was sincere, but he couldn't have
avoided what followed. The people knew something of Stalin's
sins during his lifetime, but as their father, he was forgiven.
They were children, but now they are growing up.

'Khrushchev is very unpopular. Malenkov was better—
things got a little better then, but this man is just another
gangster. Everyone calls him "Nikita the peasant", "our fat-
man", and not a soul respects him. They tell jokes about him
all the time.

'He made a big mistake with his speech at Twentieth
Congress—by the way, the report was less than everything,
you know. It was all very well criticizing Stalin, but people

wondered what that fat *muzhik* had been doing himself during all those frightful years. At best he was a coward, but also if he and the others had known about it and had kept quiet for so long, what was to prevent them from beginning all over again? And they will, they will. *He* will. He won't be content until he governs the world.

'Personally I wish Stalin had lived—then it all would soon have been over. He would have deported all the Jews to Birobidzhan, for one thing, committed all kinds of atrocities, and—well—there would have been a revolution. Now there's a sort of political vacuum; most people feel inertia. Well, it's preferable to the dogmatism—when something new comes they will accept it eagerly and quickly.'

He thought that nothing had got better recently and that there were no prospects of its ever doing so. 'They love their power too much to give us any of it,' he said, 'and nothing short of an upheaval will achieve anything for us.' I argued with him along the lines of Kolya—that more material goods are inevitable now, more education, more freedom. It really *did* make sense to me, but he refused to agree with anything that sounded even faintly pro-Soviet.

'Even in small things—materially, the situation gets continually worse. Con-tin-ually worse,' he rolled the words off again. 'The prices keep going up: the price of a cup, for instance, has gone up in the last couple of years from five roubles to ten. My mother bought an enamel basin yesterday for thirty-three roubles. Last year they were twenty-two. Next comes cars, vodka. Television sets go down because they're useful for propaganda.' (From what I heard from others, some prices had gone up but many more had come down.)

'The government is bankrupt, that's all there is to it. They couldn't even afford the festival—the people had to pay. There was a lottery that raised 300 million roubles. And you know about the state reconstruction loans—everyone paid about ten per cent of their wages for years to the government. It was supposed to come back with dividends after a period, but in April the promissory notes were cancelled and no one gets anything back. "In the spirit of patriotism" and all that. Probably it all went for the mighty sputnik. Well, we're poor too, and that was a lot of money for us. My mother gets 450 roubles a month as a typist and that's just adequate for our food for perhaps one week and a half. None left even for a pair of socks. Yuri makes 800 more, so we manage, but you see how.' He pointed to the shabby surroundings. 'The minimum wage is 300. Of course taxes are low, and rents, by your standards, but still. What could anyone do with 300 roubles? *They* say that the average wage is 700 or 800, but there are no statistics and from what I know I think it's definitely less than 600. Stenographers start at 400, even doctors at 650. Of course I may be wrong about the average— it may be higher because of all those people on top—they look after themselves, all right.

'They're the only ones who are permitted to travel, or who can afford to. Of course we can't. Or we can, we are permitted to, that's what they say, but that's no more than another example of their hypocrisy. You can take a tourist trip, *if* you leave your family behind for hostages, *if* you can afford it. Those who are paid enough to spend money on such things are the loyal ones anyway, or opportunists. They sell themselves and their consciences to earn a lot, and naturally they like things here, so they want to come back anyway. Just in case they get strange ideas, though, they must sign a contract before they leave—that they will stay always with the tourist group, never wander more than thirty metres away from the others, and be in bed at midnight. Isn't it a fantasy? But we can go nowhere anyway, so why should we worry?

'Ah, it is a horror, this life. And things will just go on this way or get worse. The reign of terror remains much the same. They say it is over, but you cannot believe them. An example is that they still have issued no telephone books, so you cannot trace disappearances. Why are there still no books if there are no more disappearances?'

'I have seen telephone books.'

'Only incomplete ones, and very out of date, and even they

are not distributed to everyone. Most of us have to go to a special office when we want a number.'

'I heard that they've promised a full one now, for everyone.'

'Well . . . perhaps they have. So what? Anyway, it is still horrible. Look at Hungary!'

'How did you hear about Hungary?'

'Oh we all know—we all know the worst. I heard about it from the radio. Others got information from the soldiers who returned. Ah, you see, nothing stops, it just goes on. And it is difficult for us to do anything—impossible really—with all the mass communication media controlled by those gangsters. There are other things too—it is difficult to organize the peasantry, and meetings are forbidden. We can't talk to strangers privately for fear of provocateurs and spies. But the communication media—that is the first, real problem . . .' he lapsed into thought.

Yuri, his brother, who had been quiet throughout our talk, suddenly joined in.

'If we were to start a revolution here, would the Americans come and help? I suppose it would be the same as Hungary— they'd waste so much time on thinking about it and voting that we'd all be dead.' He rested his head on his hands and stared hopelessly at his glass of tea. Shura and David looked up expectantly.

I had got quite worked up over all the things Shura had said, and it took a moment for the question to come into focus. Suddenly I realized what Yuri had said. 'Isn't that what you *want*, the right to *vote*? What are you *talking* about?' They blinked.

We discussed capitalism and the United States and England, and Yuri showed me a copy of *Amerika*, put out by the United States for the Russians. It is a beautifully produced glossy magazine, which Shura said was so popular that it was almost impossible to get. I could see why, if only because it was something beautiful in a world of shoddy production. I tried to convince them that America wasn't absolutely perfect either, but they had the streets-paved-with-gold idea lodged firmly in their heads. They were also certain that absolutely everything in the Soviet Union was terrible, even after I had pointed out a number of things that impressed me.

'The tortures and inhumanities of Peter the Great's time have been preserved here, as have many other things,' Shura said. 'The very essence of the system is the same, despite the seemingly radical differences. But it is ingenious, you must admit: a new tsar, but in the name of the people! What an idea! Can this be the progression of history? Can the years of American democracy and British freedom be no more than an interlude between tyrannies? Sometimes I really think that we'll all end up as apes, swinging on trees, just as we began. Somebody will drop a bomb and there'll be only a few of us left. No one will read any more, people have stopped caring already about their brains. History will make a circle, and that will be that.'

Reeling with hundreds of conflicting ideas, I went the next day, November 7, to see the parade in commemoration of the 40th anniversary of the revolution. I got up at 6 a.m. to make my way into the centre of the city before the militiamen cordoned off all traffic. The streets were still dark. At the corner two men were hurriedly installing one last picture of Lenin on a wall. Every surface was covered with red bunting and each important building decorated with portraits of Lenin and the current Top People. I got a kick out of thinking of all the frantic last-minute effort there must have been to paint pictures of Malinowsky and get rid of the old ones of Zhukov, who had been deposed only a few days before. What could they have done with them? Saved them? Burnt them? Hidden them in an attic? With the few words of Rusian I knew by then, I tried to decipher the slogans on the red and white banners. The most common one was (translated à la Mark Twain) YES! HELLO FORTIETH ANNIVERSARY OF THE GREAT OCTOBER SOCIALIST REVOLUTION! I looked it up in my dictionary later and it made sense in Russian, but I got my particular version stuck in my head all day like a bad song.

I arrived at the National Hotel near the Kremlin at the

same time as a huge party of foreigners, there for the same reason. They looked millions of light-years away, they were people unlike any people I had ever seen. I couldn't move; I had to stand in the lobby and stare at them. How gay and alive they seemed. How beautifully dressed and sure of themselves. Now I could see why Russians were so drawn to foreigners—each one was so attractive, and each in a different way, like a box of assorted chocolates. Perhaps (probably) they were basically quite alike and dull and uninteresting, but it was well hidden. The Russians were more the other way around. And one gets so starved for beauty. . . . I could have stared for hours, like all the other Russians (I felt like a Russian then) in the lobby, but the foreigners started moving and passed me on their way upstairs. Suddenly I overheard one of them speaking to another, and was slowly surprised that I could understand—I had lived for a long time in a world where practically all the noise was incomprehensible. Then it came to me that they were *Americans*, and that *I* was an American.

I soon followed them upstairs and went to a room from which I could watch the parade. Down below the streets were still dark: shining through the blackness the red of the stars on top of the Kremlin, and the silhouettes of pinnacles and cupolas. As it grew lighter, I saw that all of Manege Square was filled with rockets and khaki trucks and huge atomic guns and missiles mounted on tanks. A little later large groups of Young Pioneers dressed in pastel uniforms with red kerchiefs around their necks started forming up outside the hotel. Scoutmaster-like men tried desperately to make the children stay in line; they coaxed and pleaded and nudged but the orderly lines became dishevelled again the second their backs were turned. Two small boys began to wrestle over the possession of a big yellow balloon. Both let go and it floated up over the square. They kept scuffling and more children joined in. In despair one of their leaders pushed his way through into the centre of the bedlam and cuffed them one; this commanded their respect and they all scurried back into formation again.

At 10 o'clock the parade began. First the guns, then the children, then hefty athletes, filed past into Red Square, where 'they' and the foreign guests stood on the roof of Lenin's and Stalin's mausoleum. It wasn't as impressive as the Chinese October 1st, when the parade had included acrobats, dragons, dancers, and spectacular floats, but still a fantastic sight. A popular procession, lasting a couple of hours, finished it off. Thousands upon tens of thousands—a quarter of a million people passed in an endless stream, cheering and overcome with enthusiasm. How could it all be true, what Shura had said? Nothing could convince me that those people weren't pleased with what they had. At any rate, I now felt less willing to base my judgment simply on a few conversations—I still understood nothing. I had to live like them, or as much as possible, for a while and try to forget about the ping-pong game.

4

A Room

THROUGH SOME MIRACLE I got a room of my own. Although the Moscow skyline is almost nothing but cranes and new silhouettes, it's practically impossible to find a place to live. The city is the showplace of the USSR, and because life is easiest there everyone wants to move in. Hence the *propiska* —the only way of controlling the situation. And a Russian from another section of the country just cannot get a Moscow *propiska*. Without it he is not legally entitled to stay, and unless he stumbles across the right black market connections he must leave again.

But even without newcomers to the city, the situation is bad enough for those already there. Except for people in high-prestige work, almost everyone suffers from lack of space. One small room usually has to do for a family, however high its rate of growth, and kitchens and bathrooms are almost always shared. The kitchens are often big, with several stoves and cupboards, but in the newer flats they are really only meant for, and adequate for, one family. Housewives run back and forth from room to kitchen, trying to find enough space to prepare food and then to transport it to their room in a still eatable condition. Since no one person or family feels responsible for the kitchen or bathroom, no one bothers, and this often results in perfectly dismal conditions in the communal rooms. In some apartment houses there is a lounge for every-

47

one's use, and the space problem is less acute, but generally it's a case of a tiny, furniture-crammed room and no alternatives.

Usually rents are negligible, only 3½ to 5 per cent of the income, but it is possible to buy a black market room or apartment—if you can find someone in the unlikely position of having too much space, willing to let off part of it. This can add up to a thousand per cent of the normal rent, however, and few can afford it. So they wait to be given a new one through the normal channels—their places of employment—or, if not a new one, perhaps the old apartment of someone important enough to deserve a new one. In the meantime they must put up with complete lack of privacy and the dissension it inevitably causes. The conditions were so ghastly that I sometimes wondered how family life survived at all. Though perhaps it also provided a unifying influence. As someone aptly put it: 'Socialism and adultry are incompatible—because of the housing shortage.'

Some people I met seemed to exist entirely on the one motive force of finding a new flat. One friend who was typical lived in a room about the size of a hall cupboard. Her husband died in the war and the room was more or less adequate for her and her son, although at night when the beds were unfolded there was no floor space and they had to walk on the beds. She married again when her son was fifteen and the new husband, who may well have married her to get somewhere to live himself, moved in with them. Despite the huge shortage of men, I gathered that any girl with a room could have a choice of thousands. This marriage was on the rocks in no time almost entirely because of lack of space, but they all had to continue to stay together, and she developed an obsession about somewhere to live. After eleven years she still had nowhere to move to, and the only thing that kept her going was a dream about the home she would make some day. 'It's going to be beautiful,' she sighed dreamily, 'so beautiful. I shall make the furniture myself, and have beautiful pictures, and I shall make it so wonderful that it will be a castle. Just my own little room. I'll come home and feel that I've found my nest, I'll rest and just look at it, and love it. It will be my haven, I won't have to be afraid of anything—I will be safe, and surrounded by beauty.'

One man I knew had been happily married for fifteen years, and then his mother-in-law moved into the city when her husband died, and had to live with them because she couldn't get a room. She caused such misery in their home that within a year he couldn't stand it any more, and he asked his wife for a divorce simply to get rid of her mother. The wife subsequently married again and left with their daughter, but the mother-in-law stayed. She still had nowhere else to go, and her *propiska* was for that address. Their room is divided down the middle by a curtain, and they haven't spoken in three years. He is looking for another wife—a woman with a room.

These poor people have no time to think about the country they live in, or whether it's good or it's bad. Many are like that, as they would be anywhere in the world, and as they certainly would be in Moscow no matter what the régime.

Anyway, I got a room, a *huge* room, and felt as though I'd won the Irish Sweepstake. I had been staying with an English journalist's family, as the publishing house hadn't been able to find a place for me, but at last one of the rooms assigned to them for their employees was VACANT! It was about seventeen square metres and furnished with a bed, desk, wardrobe, cabinet, round table, and seven chairs. When I had nothing else to do I used to wonder about the various reasons someone could have had for giving me seven chairs. None of them was comfortable. Certainly not beautiful. A banquet? Musical Chairs? A dancing girl on the round table with an audience of seven?

The window was the focal point of the room. Sun beamed in all day long, and I could see the whole of the city. The tenth-floor view had everything that Moscow has: it wasn't beautiful, but it was exciting. The horizon was a continuous silhouette of unearthly looking skyscraper pinnacles, onion domes, and giant cranes putting up new buildings everywhere.

The nearest crane was immediately outside, hovering over half of a new metro station. Once in a while it flung itself around and I assumed it must have been accomplishing something, but the metro station never appeared to expand in any direction. Every day I anxiously checked its progress, longing for that wonderful time when I could walk outside and get on a train, but there didn't seem much to see but the same old skeleton dotted with ant-men.

Back from the main street, on the other side of the view, hundreds of small black huts huddled in the snow as they must have done for centuries. They were just the same as the ones in Siberia, or the ones on the outskirts of Moscow, sitting in an unpaved space which must have been a sea of mud in the spring but was now deep in snow. Not one hundred yards from the door of my modern apartment house a hand water-pump supplied the people living around it.

I shared a flat with a pretty Greek girl who had the room next to mine. There were many Greek refugees in Moscow, and they *all* seemed to be on the other side of the wall, laughing and singing warm Mediterranean music. It kept reminding me how different the Russians were. They didn't have much to laugh about, I discovered from one who spoke English—they wanted to go home, but couldn't without facing prison. The girl had fought in the Grecian mountains during the guerrilla warfare there from 1946 to 1949, when she was barely twenty. She married one of the men in the mountains, and had been with him for eight months when he was arrested; she and many of the others escaped to Russia. He had been in jail for eleven years and she hardly remembered him, but she lived for him and for something they had both believed in, with little hope for either.

Presiding over our flat was a tiny toothless old *babushka* named Dunya, who lived next door, and who cleaned, laundered and shopped for us and made endless incomprehensible speeches in Russian. I took on far more than I could handle the day I tried to teach her some English. I started with O.K. She finally mastered 'awkeh' after an overwhelming effort, and said it to everyone, all the time, and laughed and laughed and laughed.

There are all kinds of western theories about such things as the Russians' inability to manufacture plugs for sinks and baths. They're making progress: if it was once wholly true that there were none, it is only half true now. Only the sink had no plug. Another one of these little gimmicks that made Soviet life interesting was the fact that they hadn't yet achieved a key-copying machine. Three keys only were supplied with our lock, and they had to be carefully juggled and scheduled between the Greeks, Dunya, and me. If one were lost, you could try to have it copied. That took about a week, and the result never fitted the door. You could then take it back and demand satisfaction any number of times, but never with more success than the first. The solution was to have the lock taken out of the door and a new one installed, with its three keys. This was quite a regular occurrence, and meant, if you weren't prepared, coming home and finding your key had suddenly stopped working. It was an awful shock the first time, but then it became part of life.

One really baffling thing about my building, and all the others, was the elevator. It went up but not down. No matter what happened, if you broke your leg and couldn't walk down ten flights of stairs or if you had a trunk to transport to the bottom, you couldn't ride down without being subjected to a stream of abuse from the woman who sat knitting at the elevator's side on the ground floor. She was there to turn the key to get the elevator down again every time someone went up; there were no keys on the other floors, without the key you couldn't open the door, and it was taken away at night so that then there was the up climb as well. There were 188 steps up to the tenth floor, and another interesting point was that it seemed as if no two of them were the same size. At the beginning I crashed down them, and up when necessary, until it occurred to me that I really could break a leg. No one could ever explain to me why so many people were employed getting elevators down. Sergei said they were all spies who reported to the police about who went where when with whom; but if they were spies surely they could have been used for something more effective, and anyway how could there be space to store all those meaningless schedules?

I fell asleep every night to the accompaniment of Greek music, and the laughter and shrieks of any of the Greeks, or their Greek-speaking Russian friends, who happened to be staying there that night setting up cots in the next room, in the hall, in the bathroom, or anywhere there was a gap. Somehow they were always at it full blast by the time I woke up again, or maybe they never stopped, I could never figure it out. Dunya came in at eight-thirty and told them to be quiet or they'd wake me up, then she'd take off her felt boots and patter about the kitchen in her stockings. By the time she got to the kitchen the uproar would have again reached its former intensity, and she'd come out and tell them less politely to be still. Back she went to the kitchen, a crescendo of noise, and then she'd yell louder than any of them, 'ZATKNEETYE' (Shut up). This was usually what woke me up, and the same scene was re-enacted morning after morning.

The sun shone through the window and I lay there listening to the music and trying to find faces in the weird brown scrolly design of the wallpaper. After the first week there wasn't quite as much sun; Dunya was worried about the cold and came in the room every few minutes muttering and shaking her head. 'Kholodno, kholodno,' she would say, it's cold, and make a clucking noise. Finally she appeared one day with an armful of newspapers and a pan of hot glue, and set to work with great determination pasting strips of paper over all the edges of the panes, to keep out the wind. The wind had never bothered me, what there was of it, but she took this project of hers so seriously that I was left helplessly gaping. It kept out a lot of light, the room got warmer, and it was interesting to look at the newspapers as I worked at my desk— some were in English, some Russian, some Greek.

Anyway, there I was in bed with the sun shining in, and then I got up and made my way through those Greeks still spread around in the hall and joined some more in the kitchen. The food they ate was good, delicately flavored and prettily served, which was another thing that kept me conscious of the difference of Russians. The usual Russian breakfast is some kind of porridge, *kasha*, or leftover meat, or cold cuts or cheese, with bread and strong tea. Usually it's a big meal because dinner might not be for eight or nine hours. Dinner is very erratic; everyone eats it when they feel like it, and in one family it might vary from day to day from 1 p.m. to 6 p.m. with supper a few hours later. This seemed good to me—it makes no one very dependent on meals and schedules, and people have less tendency to get bogged down over the more petty details of living. But it can become awkward if one is making more than one visit in an afternoon, because there is no way out of having a dinner at each place. Russian hospitality is like that, and no one will listen to the pleas about how many dinners there have already been; in fact any refusal whatsoever on a guest's part simply breaks the hostess's heart. The food is good, but heavy and fat or doughy. Cabbage does not appear recognizably as cabbage, it becomes cabbage pie. Meat is usually fried and vegetables are scarce. Always lots of potatoes and bread, and big rich soups before every meal, and the lot smothered in *smetana* (sour cream). Naturally everyone is, by Western standards, overweight, but few people mind or go on diets. It keeps them warm in the winter, they say, and their idea of beauty is different anyway. Any normal Westerner is considered unhealthy. I was undernourished they said, and fed me more.

Except in homes and restaurants I drank *kefir* all the time and wished I hadn't eaten so much the last time I was in a home or restaurant. *Kefir* is a type of fermented milk tasting like a cross between buttermilk and yogurt. Dunya went absolutely mad when I had nothing but that. She had become hen-like and maternal to me quite soon, and this upset her utterly. She would wave her hands in the air, make speeches, all to no avail. Not only was I obstinate, but poor, she thought. She started sneaking some of the Greeks' food for me when they weren't looking, or buying bread and butter and sausages on the sly, which she cooked and presented to me as a *fait accompli*; they had to be eaten, and no two ways about it. So in the end there was just nowhere for me to go where I wasn't plagued to eat eat eat. The only thing to do was gain fifteen pounds, which I did, and then they let me alone. Dunya, anyway, would stand over me with her arms folded trying to look tough, though she wasn't much taller than me sitting down and her face was the same Slavic type as David's —covered with laugh wrinkles. She simply could never understand these crazy foreigners.

I tried to do my own shopping for a while, but it took ages, and anyway I became too susceptible to intimidation by the women in the shops. All the stores were easy to reach; in all the new buildings, the ground floor of each is a store—a *gastronom* (groceries) with dummy food models in the window; a bakery, selling every conceivable kind of delicious bread and a big assortment of quite good cakes and pastries; a dairy, with many more sorts of milk products than I knew existed—all kinds of cream, sour, sweet, thick or not, sweet pastes, curds, etc, being ladled out into the customers' containers, huge slabs of butter and cheese sold by grams, and sometimes eggs; a fruit and vegetable store, with extremely expensive fruit, usually one or two varieties, compote—mixed dried fruit, and not very good bottled vegetables and fruit; an *apteka* (chemist); a fish and meat shop; a hairdresser and barber; sometimes gift shops and others. To keep the food clean, all the saleswomen wear white uniforms, and that is also the reason for the display of cardboard or wooden food, instead of real food, in the windows, and why the cash desks are separate from the food counters. But this payment system means an infinite number of queues to wait in, sometimes for the purchase of one simple item: first to find out the price, next to pay, next to return with the receipt and get whatever-it-is, and sometimes, in the case of something slightly under or overweight—if it was impossible to weigh out exactly one kilo of oranges, for instance—back to the cash desk queue, pay a few kopecks more, get a new receipt, and again to the goods counter. Wow. If one wanted more than one thing, quite a lot of arithmetic and various calculations were involved, and far too much Russian for me to cope calmly. So Dunya eventually did most of it. She could hardly read and write, and took hours laboriously adding up the roubles and kopecks she had spent on her purchases, sitting at the kitchen table, counting aloud and marking huge crude numbers on scraps of paper bags. After she had figured it out she beamed triumphantly and went over it all to me as she placed each kopeck in my hand, awkeh.

One day someone gave me a book of photographs of pre-revolutionary Moscow, and I showed it to her because I thought she'd remember. She was overwhelmingly pleased, cooing and clucking as she saw something familiar. Then she saw a photo of the old skyline, and suddenly went to pieces. I looked at her to see what was the matter and a large tear was rolling down her cheek. 'The churches, look at all the churches, and now look!' she waved her hand at the view of Moscow outside the window. She cried and cried, and was quite overcome for the rest of the day.

Dunya was the only person I met who was religious. She wore two crosses around her neck, had an icon corner in her room, went to church every day, and wrapped her life, and thoughts of approaching death, around her religion. The thing that distressed her so much was that so few people cared anymore, and virtually all who did were of her generation. Many onion-topped towers are now no more than skeletons; many more have been converted into living space. Those that have some sort of congregation remain open, however, and the monasteries recruit as many young men as ever, from what I heard.

I was passing a church one morning when a service was going on, and went inside to see. It was in beautiful condition; outside the cupolas shone pale blue and silver, and the interior was full of very old and lovely icons. Everyone there except the priest, who had the young, handsome bearded face of an icon saint himself, was over fifty, and most a good deal older than that. They were all women, swaying, kneeling, knocking their heads on the stone floor. When I came in the priest was chanting a prayer and swinging incense, but when he looked up and saw me he hesitated and all the women turned to look. They smiled and patted me, and afterwards all gathered around to talk to me. I didn't say anything and presumably they didn't know for a while that I wasn't Russian, because from what I could gather of their talk they were saying how happy they were to see a young person there.

When the present generation of old women dies off, I can't see any future for religion. Unlike other Christian denominations, the Russian Orthodox Church is all ritual. It offers no solutions to real and current problems, nor does it even attempt to produce new ideas to capture the young's enthusiasm. Those young seek intellectual leadership above all, and regard the Church as archaic, superstitious, and useless.

Sometimes I understood what people were saying to me, and after many weeks of very hit-or-miss getting around, I picked up enough through osmosis or something for everyday conversations. At the beginning I studied, and vaguely kept it up, but doing it in an organized fashion defeated me rather early. I remember when: it was the day I discovered that there were twenty-six different ways of saying 'one'. Too many people spoke English, and I couldn't work up enough guts. To go on with, there were several all-purpose words which seemed to convey most things. *Khorosho* was a good one, for any form of approval. My favorite was *nichevo*, which could indicate practically anything: 'nothing of the kind', 'never mind', 'not bad', 'it doesn't matter', 'nothing', 'so what', and various assorted negatives ranging everywhere.

It wasn't so bad being in a country and not speaking much of the language. Strangers were terribly intrigued, because that doesn't happen in Moscow, and everyone was very kind to me if I were lost or anything. Taxi drivers went wild with excitement and frustration—they wanted to know everything about me and it was a while before I could tell them much, or understand much. It's unusual not being able to understand for months and *months*; you feel sometimes almost as if you don't exist, become somewhat deaf (all sound is like background music), and at home afterwards you just can't hear irrelevancies any more. Also you become a terrific actor.

The only thing missing from my life was news, but soon even that seemed more of a relief than a lack. I saw translations of the Russian press now and then and was quite happy not to be able to read it all the time. It was like being hit with a huge sludge of boredom. They just hacked away at you with such complete lack of subtlety that I couldn't see how they were read at all. News was late or incomplete, very little about the rest of the world except below-the-belt criticism, and pages and pages of unbelievably tedious propaganda. It all sounded exactly the same, as if they had a sausage machine and everything went in one end and came out a sausage. Russians did read them, and many at least carried them around; a newspaper was a useful article, and could fill many needs that might arise. It could be used as wrapping paper, or a corner for a jotted note, or toilet paper, or to protect either end of the anatomy in case of rain: over the head, or between you and the wet park bench.

I had mail, which told me something. After I moved it came very irregularly, sometimes in a week, sometimes two months. There seemed to be some difficulty about my name being registered, but this was one mystery that I never came near solving. When for a number of weeks no mail came to my new address, but turned up instead at the publishing house, at the old address, and even at the American Embassy —though there was nothing but the new address on any of the letters and no clues that could possibly have indicated these other destinations—I tried to find out what the trouble was. Apparently, I was told by one of the resident foreigners, it was necessary to register my address with the main post office, who had a list of people whose mail from abroad was supposed to be delivered promptly. So I went to the official who deals with such matters, whose reaction was one of unbelief and amazement. 'List? What list? We have no list!' Nothing much changed after that, except that now and then a few letters came where they were directed. The rest continued to land all over town.

'We have no censorship' either. Sometimes the envelopes were full of damp glue and the letters had to be pried open. Still, I preferred knowing, and was happy that Soviet technology hadn't reached American heights, and they had no machine capable of X-raying letters undetected.

Occasionally I went to the library and read the New York papers, months late but it didn't really matter considering how far behind and away I was. Stories about Moscow seemed far more plentiful than I'd ever realized, and after reading them, the other news, the sports, the theatre and book reviews, I was projected right back into their atmosphere. I couldn't believe it, I simply couldn't, when I went out the door and found myself in Red Square looking at the Kremlin.

The stories about Russia didn't always seem much more accurate than the Russian stories on America, but at least they were subtle. Russians weren't allowed to read them; I had to prove my foreign identity. Overwhelming everyone was an utter lack of contact with the outside world, and sometimes it seemed amazing to think that there was an outside world, that Moscow wasn't a thing in itself, an island. No books came over, no magazines, no news (except for people who understood a foreign language well enough to listen to the BBC or the Voice), no evidence that *this* wasn't the whole world.

5

A City

I'VE BEEN TRYING to remember what I thought Moscow was like before I lived there. Something dark and mysterious, I think, filled with swarms of grey peasants and workers, none of them with faces. A place as remote as the moon, but less interesting. I hope other people have different ideas, because mine were wrong. I knew that quite soon, but it took a lot of exploration and existing to discover the city's personality.

It seemed to hide itself, under trees in the summer and snow in the winter, under quietness, and under anonymous buildings, stores with impersonal numbers, and five million interchangeable people. It had some beauty: churches, the Kremlin, some of the early nineteenth-century buildings; and quite a lot of ugliness: the newish skyscrapers and the miles of Bronx-like apartment houses. For one of the world's biggest cities, some of it was archaic: the broken-down wooden houses and often outdated methods of building replacements; but some of it easily surpassed Western cities in the modern conception of a metropolis: the air and lightness everywhere, cleanliness, the grand width of the streets. It is a long-isolated city which has reached many of the same twentieth-century ends as its counterparts elsewhere, but in its own way.

I had a lot of free time to spend on both the people and the place: the latter necessarily, because I lived a long way from anywhere I had to go. Moscow is built in concentric cycles, and the transportation system is a spider with its body in the middle. To get from one place to another one must usually go in on bus or metro, then change direction out again. As a result, one gravitates to the centre, a space of about four large blocks, and can almost count on meeting a friend in the crowds pushing across the streets. Also because of this, the best places to live are near the centre, and that is what people want rather than any particular section of town. Moscow is the only city I've seen where no residential district is more, or less, desirable; where you can't tell anything about someone just by his address. There are no slum, bohemian, or 'smart' sections.

The pre-revolutionary city, three-quarters of which was wooden and more than half single-storied, is disappearing. Only the more solid and pretty of the old mansions and palaces remain for good, and many of them have been picked up and moved to widen the streets. Most of the post-revolutionary buildings are like frosted cakes, ghastly and rather Victorian, except for one or two glass and concrete blocks built during the 'thirties. Stalin's yen for skyscrapers crushed these beginnings of modern architecture—there are six skyscrapers, dominating the view in every direction, thirty-odd floors of pinnacled glory each. Khrushchev disapproves of the waste (since Moscow's base is clay, not rock, their foundations alone were enormous undertakings, and maintenance costs are exorbitant too), so no more will be built. Meanwhile I still ran into people who resolutely defended them; the division between those who did and those who didn't had no relation to taste, only to politics. 'One must consider the whole,' said the defenders, 'the line of the new buildings must correspond with the old. Look at the Lenin Library [of fairly modern and attractive design and construction] from a distance, and you see how it jars on the eye. But the skyscrapers! Ah, majestic, strong, and just our Russian style!'

Every morning, after some work was done, my expedition into the city began. Padded with so many sweaters, jackets and coats that I could have rolled down the ten flights of stairs, I would smile rather unenthusiastically at the woman at the bottom (who never smiled back after the time I went downstairs, knowing no better, and brought the elevator up to get a huge stack of books down)—then out to face the cold. It was absolutely terrifying sometimes, crashing into you with the force of an explosion. A Muscovite has enough to do simply dealing with nature, regardless of anything else. From the time of the first snowfall at the end of October it rarely stops for more than a day or two, and the temperature is always freezing. During some cold spells it goes down to twenty or thirty below and stays there, and if there is wind of any kind, simply going outside is sheer agony. I sometimes felt as if I were going to disintegrate, it hurt so much—I thought pieces of me would begin to change form from solid to gas, and atoms would detach themselves and float away.

The children playing in the courtyard adored its compensations too much to care. They were there in multitudes at all hours, making everything out of snow, sledding where there was no slope and skating where there was no ice. They had one patch of snow which they had packed down hard, and expertly manœuvred its bumps and crevices on their skates. The Moscow children could skate on anything; even though the biggest park was completely flooded in the winter for a rink and there were smaller ones dotted all over the city, they preferred something less tame. They were good enough to manage the bumpy or melting snow they could find any-where—even the paths through the ring of parks around the city were constantly full of them, running and sliding and laughing.

Destination One was the bus stop. The buses came very frequently, but there was always a queue and usually a free-for-all to get on. Apparently the queue is fairly recent; Muscovites used to be less civilized about it. Now, anyway, they wait in a disciplined and polite way—until the bus comes; it stops and when the doors open several people nearly fall out of the back. 'Move to the front, citizens! A little more, *please!'* bellows the conductor. The old people and children get on at the front where special seats are reserved for them; otherwise the front door is the exit. The rest of us battle our way in the rear. Among all those getting on at the same stop a sort of loyalty develops, and we all help each other to squeeze in or just to get a hand-hold on a bar. Even though the more there are the more uncomfortable it is, we're on the same team. But the next stop—ah, that queue is on another side altogether, and not the least effort is made to help them in. So the *'Move* to the front, citizens!' again.

There is a sort of custom about lucky tickets. The conductor hands them out, to those she can reach, then follows rapt scrutiny of their tickets by the riders. If the first three digits of your number add up to the same total as the last three, you'll be lucky all day.

In the winter all the windows freeze into a solid layer of frost and ice, and no one, except the conductors with instinct, knows where the bus is. The only thing you can tell is exactly how cold it is, by the depth of the frost layer. Or if you get a seat, ho-ho, you can see through the peephole. Early in the morning, when the bus first started making its rounds and while the windows were still transparent, the first passenger beside each one started rubbing a tiny hole through the thin beginning of ice. It's almost a sacred obligation to continue the peephole, and the next person in the seat takes off his glove for one freezing instant to clear it again. Children make big ones, or scratch designs, or make patterns with kopeck coins, on the windows near the front seats.

Once on, and your stop identified, the biggest trick is to get out again. The conductor takes the money and gives out tickets, constantly urging people forward like a broken record even if another inch forward on anyone's part would make the front of the bus fall out. You have to, anyway, to be able to make an exit at the stop you had in mind. But despite a fine if you were caught getting out at the rear, I found that it was the only way I could do it at all, so I tried to stay small and invisible near the door. Otherwise there were all sorts of sardine-like gymnastics needed, plus a large and pungent Russian vocabulary, to work your way forward.

The ride is made more interesting in the case of trolley-buses. An ear-splitting thunderous crash could be expected, the original Chicken Little's falling sky, even if the journey was otherwise uneventful. The driver had just got a little over-exuberant in a race with a taxi and the cable had slipped from the overhead wires. Everyone would get out to advise and supervise the effort at re-connection, all traffic would stop, and gaping crowds gather. The frequency of this occurrence damped no one's interest.

Russian men are rarely rude in crowded buses, but also rarely polite enough to give up their seats. Women are equals and that is that. Once in a while a beggar would get on, moaning about his war injuries and the unjustness of the world. Or sometimes drunks who started rows, or a pleasant one with an accordion who got everybody swaying and humming to his tune. And many times people seemed to make friends, or one person said something funny and following the general laughter somebody else told a story, and the conductor started calling them 'comrades' instead of 'citizens'. These things weren't the general rule, but something always happened to teach me more about Russians, and I loved taking these rides except when I was primarily interested in getting somewhere. Thinking of the English and the French, maybe one can learn a lot about a country by riding on its buses.

The metro was Destination Two, and it took me where I needed to go or to another bus, or a tramcar, or the start of a good long walk, or all three. The Moscow metro had less human attraction than the buses, but couldn't have had a consistently more beautiful performance, and beautiful surroundings for those who like that sort of thing. The Muscovites do; they were horrified at my suggestion that the metro might have gone further if all the money hadn't been spent on chandeliers, friezes, mosaics and marble. It will soon go further anyway, they say. Thirty-four stations had been

built, each entirely different, most of them decorated in palatial splendour, but some more simply and attractively. There
are no slot-machines, and few signs—you recognize the stops
mainly by the decorations. The whole affair runs with 21st
Century perfection. The trains seem to glide on ball bearings
with hardly a jolt or a rumble, they come all the time and on
time, a voice from nowhere announces each stop and the next
one, everything is kept spotless by platoons of hard-polishing
women, and everyone behaves very well. It just wasn't as
much fun.

The first thing at the top of the metro escalator was always
an ice-cream stand. Stout women in white overalls stood behind small counters selling five or six different kinds, and
people bought and ate it even if there were twenty degrees of
frost. Nearby would be an upright shoe-shine stand, covered
with inner soles, polish, and shoe laces of all colours. The
men and women who tend these stands, I was told, are all
Assyrian refugees from Iraq, and have the only monopoly
there is. There are many more street vendors everywhere,
selling pink water, *pirozhki* (hot pastry stuffed with egg, rice,
or meat), tobacco, flowers, magazines, books. They don't
make any noise or any effort, as one somehow expects.

The streets always seemed very hushed and quiet to me,
though maybe it was because of my Russian-deafness. But
horns aren't honked, just as in Paris and Rome, vendors don't
vend (out loud at least), I never heard bells ring, and rarely
an animated conversation, so there must be something in it.
Only on a holiday or election day is there a perfectly colossal racket, with loudspeakers above every corner crackling with
choruses of folk songs or Soviet pops.

The streets are also relatively colourless in the winter, and
so are the people. They move along solidly and gravely in
their sombre-coloured coats, not looking at each other. Sometimes pedestrians stopped me to ask where they were or where
I had bought my shoes, but most of the time they hurried to
attend to their business and get out of the cold. From the way
they were dressed, they seemed to fit fairly evenly into cate-

gories. But except for the children, and the more sophisticated *stiliagi* and their chic molls, their clothes were almost uniformly hideous. Many were peasant-looking, the men in frayed sheepskin or quilted coats, the women in grey padded jackets, *valenki* (high felt boots), and shawls. Slightly higher up were shoddy cloth coats, still the shawl but sturdy shoes instead of *valenki*. Highest of all were hats and fur or fur-trimmed coats. The children were all in the highest bracket. Each one, especially the smallest, was so smothered in fur that only its face peeped out, and it looked like a fluffy pom-pom rolling down the street. Their clothes are cheaper, and all children are marvellously well cared-for anyway. They are the best dressed, best fed, best entertained, best everything. They represent the future.

Everywhere there is scaffolding surrounding the shells of new buildings, and on the walls advertisements of the latest movies or concerts, and panels with all the newspapers displayed on them. A few people stand around reading the papers, or a queue waits for a movie or a store to open (dinner hour for storekeepers is as vague as anyone else's, and without inside information you can't tell which hour any one store is shut). They all cross the street with no more than a perfunctory glance at the oncoming traffic. I never saw an accident but there seemed to be a near miss on the average of every other minute. For the country that is alleged to have the stiffest driving test (requiring complete knowledge of the insides of cars and a thorough physical examination—eyes, heart, back, feet—as well as considerable skill at driving) the actual situation is terrifying. Drivers speed and swerve and stall, and exhibit no more concern for the pedestrians than vice versa. It's all a sort of elaborate sport, of who-can-nearly-run-over-whom, or who-can-nearly-make-who-think-he's-just-run-over-me. If a car is coming a hundred yards away and some amateur judges he can make it across the six-lane street before it catches up with him, he soon realizes the error of his ways, because quite often the oncoming car seems deliberately to speed up and try its best to hit him. He runs like mad and escapes, but he's lost that round. Eventually he learns the other game though—ha! so he thinks he's got me scared, does he? Well, I'll just keep going slowly, slowly . . . With a jangling screech the driver brakes an inch away and curses with great screamings and wavings of arms. The pedestrian has won that one, and proceeds with his smug indifferent smile, as if he can't really imagine what all that non-cultured commotion is about.

For all that, driving offences are severely punished. Three offences are allowed—such things as speeding, overtaking on a hill—and after that the licence is lifted. There's almost always someone there to catch you—to mark one third of your license. With a smile. Even having a *dirty* car is fined. And there are all kinds of unexpected snags in the Moscow traffic layout. For instance, at some main intersections to turn left you have first to turn right, proceed ahead, make a U-turn, go back the way you came, cross the intersection again, and presto. On many corners there are four traffic lights to complicate things further, two reds and two greens, any combination of which can mean something entirely different. And militiamen supervising them who can change it all around any old way besides.

If no one else can, some of the taxi drivers at least figure out what it is all about. The taxi drivers are closer to their New York counterparts than anything else—sarcastic and friendly, sometimes real smart-alecs. When I was able to talk to them a little, though, I found many of them had a lot under that surface and were filled with curiosity and astounding knowledge of cultural and political subjects. But the one thing none of them did know was Moscow geography. They could master the corners and beat the lights, but without explicit instructions for every inch of the route they couldn't find anything. Quite often, if I knew nothing more about my destination than its address, we went on wild goose chases all over the town. The driver's object in the end became simply one man in the street who knew, but none of them did either. The fare kept mounting, but it was always a fascinating hunt. Unfortunately they loved to race, and try out other ingenious experiments to escape the tedium of driving properly; perhaps the reason they didn't know Moscow was because they lost their licences and jobs so frequently that the turnover was high.

There are taxi-stands all over the city: rows of checker-striped Pobedas, Volgas, sometimes a cheaper Moskvich or more expensive Zil (it used to be Zis, but the S for Stalin became L for Likhachev, the director of the factory making them), with the drivers reading or asleep behind the wheel. It was rarely difficult to find one, but on busy nights the taxis in the stands were joined by private drivers trying to make some extra money. They hadn't the licence for it and it was against the law, but practically impossible to control. In fact, most of them were the chauffeurs of important people, using their bosses' cars and charging whatever they could get.

It seemed as if almost everyone who had a car had a driver to go with it, whose only job was to come when called, drive where asked, and sit and meditate outside until it was time to go home again, missing meals and consuming hours of what might have been either productive labour or leisure. Whenever I heard speeches about the conspicuous waste of labour, or class labour, or exploitation, under capitalism, I thought about them. But the drivers get their own back, supplementing their incomes in certain established and devious ways. One is the part-time taxi work. Another is the buying of petrol from truck drivers at reduced rates and charging the boss the full price. Trucks get a discount on fuel, and a larger ration quota, so their drivers buy all they're entitled to and sell the surplus—to the profit of everyone except the people running the show.

Quite a number of Muscovites own cars, and after China, where there were so few, all of Moscow seemed a traffic jam. A car is expensive, though, and even if someone can afford one he has to wait about three years before his name reaches the top of the priority list. When it does, when he has that car, he really loves it, and he pats it, coaxes it, trains it. One interesting sidelight, either on the acute lack of spare parts or on general dishonesty, is that he never leaves the wind-shield wipers on. When it rains they are brought out, but at home taken off and stowed inside the glove compartment. If he forgets, they're as good as gone.

Along the sides of the streets quilt-jacketed women shovel snow into heaps and hack at caked ice with long crowbars. Chop chop chop—however quiet it is, there is always that. The snow clearing is terrific; no sooner is it on the ground than people are sweeping, shovelling and hacking. When it is all in even piles along the gutters the big snow-eaters come along and cart it away. These machines are so enthralling that they draw top audiences wherever they go. They look like the invention of a child, because their conception seems to be more human than mechanical. There is a simply enormous shovel sticking down at a thirty-degree angle with a driver's cab under the handle part of it. On the scoop of the shovel are two arm-like things with hands to push the snow on and up to a rotary belt that conveys it to the top and heaps it into a dumptruck waiting underneath. Then it is thrown into the Moscow River or through manholes into the sewers. In an average winter week, a quarter of a million tons of snow are cleared like this. Most of the street workers are women, big husky ones who keep busy in the summer sweeping with twig brooms. Others are people being punished for misdemeanours, sentenced to a day or a week of shovelling to increase their public spirit.

I rarely saw dogs or cats in the streets, and gathered that relatively few people had pets and that there were no strays. There seemed to be very few animals altogether—no ducks on ponds and almost no pigeons. But they are very kind to the pigeons they do have. In the city centre, outside the building of the Council of Ministers, there is a roped-off patch of sidewalk daily covered with crumbs.

The best stores in the Soviet Union, I was told, are the ones in the centre of Moscow. Many are attractively decorated, particularly perfume and confectionery stores, and gift shops for tourists. These sell handicrafts from the fifteen republics of the USSR, China and Eastern Europe: embroidered blouses and table linen, hand-painted wooden boxes, dolls, jewellery and other knick-knacks and trinkets. All of them were expensive, but they were the only objects I could find on sale that were well-made and attractive.

Other specialty shops sell furs, flowers, cosmetics, dietetic foods, leather goods and so on. The leather one, the best I suppose in the country, didn't have a black belt. I went back time and again, and finally settled for a brown one long enough to have belted me perpendicularly and horizontally, with bows, like a Christmas present. I tried everywhere to buy gloves, but each pair available was about three inches too long and an inch too narrow. Does anyone have hands like that? In the end I had to buy some giant brownish mittens and shorten the thumb and mitt until they fitted.

The stocks of most necessities were usually adequate; there was never a question of freezing, just the eternal battle against the appalling quality and expense. The only serious quantity problem seemed to arise over furniture. With so many people moving into new flats or just trying to furnish what they had attractively, there was much more demand than supply. One furniture store that I passed regularly was always bare, so that I assumed it had gone out of business. One day I saw two trucks outside and men carting things in, and I stopped to watch this event. The cargo was glass-fronted bookcases, so many that when they were all unloaded they filled the store to overflowing. Within a few days they were gone and the shop was bare again.

All over the city are the state commission shops that buy and sell second-hand goods, taking 12½ to 15 per cent on the exchange. People go to them to sell one object for another, or to pick up something rare or foreign that may have found its way there. They often have a sizeable collection of very peculiar and ancient white elephants, as well as an occasional bargain with a mysterious background. A girlfriend of mine found some bright-checked slacks with a Selfridge's label in them. Many go the commission shop rounds first, but, if unlucky, must proceed to the department stores.

Gum, among the world's biggest stores, is the famous one. Off-hand, I can't think of anything that has ever depressed me more. Its name stands for *Gosudarstveni Universalni Magasin*, state universal store, and it sits opposite the Kremlin like a huge crouching living thing, ready to thwart any and all comers. The window displays are amateur, but there is little worth showing in them anyway. One window, though, is often filled with unobtainable foreign imports or futuristic Soviet merchandise, and passing people jam the sidewalk to see. Inside it is huge and stone, with two tiers and three alleys of almost separate shops. In the centre of its cavernous depths is a big fountain, and sometimes seasonal decorations—a Chrismas tree, or Uncle Frost (Father Christmas) for the New Year. And thousands of frustrated shoppers, and hundreds of utterly rude, sullen, and apathetic saleswomen and cashiers, who sit there just daring you. I'm sorry I can't give an objective, unemotional description; I am prejudiced because of my quite unreasonably intense hatred of the place.

Having left home with only enough clothes for three weeks of August weather, I was in a bad way when the real cold spells began. Gum, therefore, became part of life—once a week, crash into gear for that trek, sometimes with hope but never without defeat. It never had anything at all that I needed, or if it did it demanded all my money for it. It didn't have a Russian Astrakhan hat, it didn't have a non-freakish-flowered or striped or blotchy scarf, it didn't have a piece of cardboard big enough to make a lampshade (I just couldn't manage those Russian fringed affairs), it didn't have shampoo, it didn't have the simplest things. And, besides sharing the peculiar Western habit of rarely stocking winter clothes in the winter, what it did have was too expensive and hideous. I had absolutely no right to have qualms about the ugliness considering how cold I was, but I had plenty. Even the Russians had as many qualms as they could afford: fashion displays were ignored, and week after week I returned to find them untouched. But anything imported for sale was quickly snatched up, so you had to keep going back just in case. And then there were queues and queues. Once I saw one that must have been a quarter of a mile long, threading its way through the wide Gum spaces out into the street into a procession that could have rivalled the one on the opposite side of Red Square, in front of the Lenin-Stalin mausoleum. I think Muscovites must have joined the Gum queue without a notion of what it was they were waiting for—it was bound to be imported and probably needed. At least it would be beautiful. With the relatively small amount of money allocated to consumer goods in the USSR, it seemed strange that even then so little is produced that anyone wants, as distinct from what everyone needs. Lack of taste I discounted; if the people have enough to recognize something beautiful, surely the trained designers must.

To keep from freezing I had to have a coat. I couldn't afford a Russian one, despite my generous wages, so I was airmailed one from England to the British Embassy. It got colder and colder, I made regular telephone calls to the embassy, but nothing was heard. Before long the British were as concerned as I was; inter-office memos on the subject of The Coat were flying back and forth, and everyone there seemed fully primed down to the last detail. They even offered me their coats.

Anyway, airmail or not, my coat arrived in two months. I received a notice to go to Ostankino, an almost inaccessible spot on the outskirts of Moscow where all parcels from abroad are delivered, and one terribly cold day I went out to the wilds to collect it. The customs man opened the package in front of me, and I nearly swooned at the sight of anything so wonderful and warm as my coat. He picked it up, examined it, and said: '800 roubles.' Ha-ha, he's joking, says I to myself. '800 roubles what?' 'Custom duty,' says he, looking at me strangely. I tried to explain in bits of Russian, English, and pantomime that I didn't have 800 roubles, which was in my case more than three times the value of the coat, all I had was eighty; that I'd waited two months, that it was really very cold, and surely he was a reasonable man. He understood, tried to explain something back which I didn't, shrugged his shoulders and returned the coat to its box.

In despair I went back to the city and started telephoning people who might be able to help. Nobody knew what to do, but eventually at the publishing house, when I was airing the latest instalment of my little adventure, some kind soul offered to help and worked out an official letter for me to the chief of customs. Armed with this, I went to his ministry or whatever it was, got past three different people who all said 'impossible', found a fourth who agreed to send my letter in to the chief—who actually read it, spoke on the phone for a minute, and got the coat for me for nothing.

The two things in the Soviet Union that nearly drive the uninitiated mad are bureaucracy and inefficiency, which blend into each other to such a degree that often it's difficult to place the blame when something goes wrong. They are traditional Russian specialties, legacies from years before the revolution, and very much everywhere still. My coat didn't really have much to do with it, except that I eventually got to the person willing and able to break precedent when the case was reasonable. The exorbitant customs duty had been imposed because it always is, on the assumption that the person who gets the goods will sell them for far more than they're worth, and the duty is the deterrent. The fact that I was living there, freezing, and minus 800 roubles, was entirely irrelevant to everyone but the man with enough intelligence and power to make a fresh decision. I was seeing at work some advice I had received at the beginning. Everyone just loves to say 'impossible'. The point is, it usually isn't, but you won't believe that for long unless you can get past them. Somewhere, in some little invisible cubby-hole, lives a little invisible man, the only one capable of making decisions—of lifting up the right telephone which connects with the right string. The trick is to find the man, because no one will ever tell you who it is, and it usually isn't as obvious as it was with my coat.

Though I could never tolerate the bureaucracy, I learned to live with the inefficiency. Everyone else does, though perhaps that's the trouble. Nowhere have I seen people put up with quite so much. It is such a part of life, and something they think themselves so powerless to change, that nobody worries about it. In any case, the values are different, and some of these things simply aren't important. It has probably never occurred to anybody, for instance, that it might be easier for everyone concerned (leaving out logic) if parcels addressed to Moscow could be sent to Moscow, instead of Ostankino. The ride to Ostankino gives one plenty of time to read, or to think about things that are important.

Culture for the Masses

WHAT IS IMPORTANT, and what do Muscovites think and do? All those people walking along, pushing into the bus, wandering through Gum? When they're not doing this, and not at work, then what? I wanted to do it too, whatever it was, but just as it turned out (big surprise) that there was nothing peculiar about them as people simply because they were Russians, so there was nothing very unusual about what they did with themselves either. Except perhaps for the numbers involved in higher-brow pursuits, the absence of lower-brow alternatives, and some few Russian and Soviet variations on all themes, they look for the same escapes and stimulations as anyone anywhere. The biggest difference, one of degree, is with reading. They read intelligent books, as many as they can get hold of: every Russian wants to be an egghead.

A lot of the time I seemed to end up being taken to restaurants, but this was not everyone's choice. It was the privilege only of those who could afford it, and the mecca only of those unpuritanical enough to feel they were not wasting precious time that could be used for self-improvement or other productive activity. It wasn't encouraged, and was extremely expensive by Soviet standards. An evening's bill for a full meal for two was equivalent to a street cleaner's total weekly wage. But the highly paid, or their children, had nothing much to spend their money on anyway, and once they began on this form of entertainment they seemed to become addicted. They went several times a week, sometimes for a big meal, some-times just fruit and wine, usually a good deal of alcohol; always for the whole evening, and always to be relieved of a healthy stack of roubles.

There were small, comparatively cheap restaurants, and a thin scattering of bars, patronized by the less affluent when that particularly Russian urge came on them to get drunk. I found them ashamed of drunkenness in principle, but abso-lutely unswerving when it came time to test their own alco-holic mettle. They didn't fool around with cocktail parties, or socially sipping something, or an occasional lift; when they started they attacked it with determined ferocity, as if Russia and the world depended on it. They would fill up that vodka glass, seize it with one hand and some mineral water or black bread with the other, gulp back the vodka, make a painful face, quickly drink the water, then repeat the ritual again until numbness set in. No distractions, please, this is *serious* drinking. If they really had to get drunk so madly and so unpleasantly, I suggested (once), why didn't they eliminate the dilution stage and pour it straight down from the bottle? This idea got a very unreceptive reception. They didn't want to talk about their drinking habits because they felt it exposed the latent bourgeois non-culture of the Russian. Being non-cultured was the ultimate horror. No one would take me into the more sordid of the little bars, either: 'Women don't go,' they said, 'and it is very ugly in there.' A bare layer of subtlety veiled the Russian drinker in the bigger restaurants. But they were always there to be recognized, sometimes without very much difficulty if they were unseemly enough to shout or throw something or create some kind of scene. That wasn't rare, and it covered the more sober ones with unbearable confusion until the non-cultured one was gently escorted to the door. But never did I see the Russians in a more human light. They could let themselves go and have a simply roaring fabulous binge. When vodka, always discouragingly expensive, went up at the end of the year, there were an awful lot of unhappy people. Many of them organized a boycott, and simply wouldn't buy it. Instead, there was bootleg vodka on sale by street hawkers, or people made it themselves.

Everyone wasn't like that, nor were all the restaurants. The swankiest ones were run by Intourist, had menus in French, German and English, waiters in evening dress, and a comparatively sedate atmosphere. No one was exactly falling over themselves to serve you; they expected you to sit it out for a good long time. The meals were often large enough to require that anyway. There were big soups, *zakuski*—endless varieties and helpings of hors-d'œuvre—meats, salads, cheeses, caviar, smoked salmon, eggs; then meat courses, bread and potatoes, vegetables; dessert, fruit, coffee, pastries, chocolates; and in between vodka and various kinds of Soviet wine. When they eat, they eat, and when they drink, they drink. In between and all along there were intermissions for dancing, usually a sort of mild two-step to the music of a Sovietized jazz band.

Jazz is frowned upon as it is alleged to reflect the confusion of bourgeois society, but someone will have to think of something new soon because the wedge has long since passed the thin end. I found more fanatical jazz enthusiasm in Russia than anywhere else I've been. Almost everyone loved it, if only as an expression of resentment at the ban. I even had to learn to rock 'n' roll in Moscow because I could hardly go to any young person's house without finding everyone doing it, or playing it, or at least discussing it. They listened religiously every evening to the Voice of America jazz hour, and they bought records from beeznessmen who got them—somewhere, mysteriously—or they had copies of records on X-ray plastic, or at least tape recordings. There was good jazz at some of the restaurants too—at the National Hotel (where the nearest Soviet equivalent to a 'smart young set' was going while I was there) a young group played real cool stuff nightly, even though the window beside them looked out on the Kremlin— but jive dancing in public is still taboo. A lot of people thought it would be all right soon though, because a justification had been thought of: that jazz had its origins among an oppressed American people.

None of the restaurants had soft lights or an intimate atmosphere, but this seemed to be the only thing they all had in common. The Sovietskaya contained the only bar I saw. It looked a little as if the designer had copied a picture and wasn't familiar with the normal proportions of such things— or maybe he just was an exceptionally big man. The bar seemed about seven feet high and the stools shoulder height. Mounting one was quite an athletic feat. There was a fairly good Chinese restaurant in the Peking Hotel; a very good Georgian one—Aragvi, with twangy music, moustached men and wonderful flat Georgian bread; the Praga, where the music from the band in the main room was piped to other ones, including private dining rooms which could be hired for parties; the Moscow Hotel Café, with a view of all the city; the National Café, where beeznessmen and what prostitutes there were congregated (according to Sergei); and others— Sofia, Ararat, Baku, Riga—offering specialized cooking. Despite these differences, though, an evening in one was an evening in any. People went in couples or large groups, choosing the space and light and uproar of the restaurants as an alternative to their tiny furniture-choked rooms.

Parties could only be given by those with big apartments and without the usual surfeit of relatives, and there weren't many so fortunate. But anyone who could, did, as often as space and finances would allow, and no excuse necessary. Russian hospitality is fabulous. Parties or dinners were as prolonged, clamorous and alcoholic as restaurant evenings.

Then there were films, theatre, concerts, ballet. All were cheap, all popular, and each more impossible than the last, in that order, to get tickets for. Nothing could be arranged impulsively—all seats had to be booked in advance. Some of the difficulty had a lot to do with inefficiency. Movies were extremely popular, and although Soviet films weren't always good and foreign imports were rare, everybody had to see everything that came out. The cinemas were minute stuffy boxes, but often occupied only a small part of a very big and labyrinthine building. For waiting in, there were buffets, smoking rooms, lounges, sometimes art galleries or sopranos and string quartets to keep the clients amused, and all because no one had thought of constructing an auditorium large enough to accommodate the people who, after all, only came there with one purpose: to see a movie.

Muscovites flock to the theatre in hordes, but I didn't go very often because, although the standards of production and execution were rarely less than great, I found nothing more down-dropping than an uplifting play about the achievements of Soviet Man. The public wasn't altogether untouched by this feeling, and themselves greeted a Chekhov or Mayakovsky play, or a foreign classic, with far more enthusiasm than the newer crop of socialist realist drama. Enthusiasm could be measured by the applause: not its strength or length so much as whether the audience burst spontaneously into rhythm, clapping together in time, over and over and over. There was a brilliant puppet theatre which, with its inherent limitations, couldn't and didn't try to put over a cement factory, and left propaganda alone in favour of fun. The gypsy theatre had marvellous dancing and wild spirit. And the circus, with clown Oleg Popov, a lady tiger-wrestler, acrobats and extravagant spectacle, was produced in just the right atmosphere— a small audience and only one thing going on at a time. Each time I went Khrushchev was there.

Despite jazz passion, no Russian sees any contradiction in being manic about classical music as well. I was overwhelmed by the level of sophistication of the musical public. Not that there is really a musical public, unless it includes everyone— the people at concerts were of all ages, backgrounds and circumstances, and all intensely serious. Even confirmed *stiliagi* came. Everyone is wildly proud of the part Russia has played in the world's music and of their current composers and musicians, prouder, perhaps, than of anything. The day after Shostakovich's Eleventh Symphony was performed for the first time, hardly another subject was mentioned anywhere in Moscow. It seemed to represent something essentially personal to them all, and everyone longed for it to be great. It

was impossible to imagine such an event having such significance to the ordinary people of any other country.

Most popular of all as an entertainment is ballet. The Bolshoi meant so much more than I could describe. It was such
a lot more than Western ballet—not just some people on a
stage dancing well, but an event, full of emotion and strength
and towering beauty. Its very lavishness was the main thing,
in a world where little else was: thus seeing the Bolshoi per-
form on tour in a Western city could never convey the same
effect. Every Russian is a balletomane, and there is the most
amazing competition for tickets. Before almost every performance there were mobs outside, and the path to the door was
a small obstacle course through stampeding crowds pleading
for tickets at any price. They patiently waited at the box
office every day, every week, every month. A high proportion
of the lucky ones inside, besides tourists, were from the fur-
coated set. A government official's daughter gave me an explanation for their luck—she showed me a book of passes
entitling the bearer to seats for any form of entertainment.
'Who gets those?' I asked. She held her hand up high above
her head.

Since I wasn't a tourist or important, there were problems.
There was always a chance of going with foreign visitors, but
I didn't meet many. I was never intelligent enough to think of
a solution, but one happened to me by accident. I always
arranged to meet friends outside the Bolshoi because it was
near everything, and in the beginning it was the only place I
could find or even pronounce. One horribly cold evening I
was early and went inside to wait. I began pacing up and
down the empty lobby, then noticed a doorman solemnly
watching me, his head turning back and forth, back and forth,
in time to my pacing. I asked if I was annoying him, and he
replied with grave solemnity: 'Niet.' I walked some more, his
head kept rhythm like a metronome. Eventually he got up,
went over to a counter where books and photographs were
sold, came back up to me and presented me with some picture postcards. He was still absolutely lemon-faced, and I

couldn't understand what any of it was about. He wanted to talk to me, he said then. So over the top of my Russian-English dictionary we struck up a conversation, and soon he was rocking with laughter at my absurd Russian. I had to leave soon, but whenever I saw him again he had always found me a ticket for a rare Ulanova performance or something special—or if a ticket was impossible, at least some more pictures.

People trekked out to all these things, through the snow, shoes in hand and boots on feet. Each building had a cloak-room surrounded by scrambling women, changing their shoes, being dismantled of layers of coats, and trying to comb the tangles out of their permanents. Before performances or during intermissions they made their way to the buffets for beer or champagne or something to eat, or to the theatre museum, or to the inevitable room where couples and groups walked around and around and around in circles. No one could give me its history, nor the explanation of why they always walked counter-clockwise.

One of the first things all Westerners notice in Moscow is the enormous book-reading public: the taxi driver and the waitress waiting for customers, the customers themselves, everybody and always. They read while walking along or (of course) while crossing the street, while standing in queues or even for the twenty seconds of an elevator ride. The biggest crowds anywhere are in bookshops, and the tiny sidewalk bookstalls do a roaring business even in the foulest weather. All this is encouraged: books are cheap, editions astronomical (the number of books published annually far exceeds that of any other country), and reading, anyway, is an always available escape. But the hunger for ideas is so powerful among any people traditionally kept subordinate by their lack of knowledge, as the Russians were throughout history, that very little encouragement is needed. Seeing this on such a mass scale is miraculous to visitors from countries where people think there's something wrong with you if you read, or if you do you must limit it to thrillers or sexy best-sellers.

Ilya Ehrenburg, one of the top contemporary Soviet writers, discussed this during a seminar at the youth festival. 'A cultured public has been created in the Soviet Union. The point is not the number of outstanding writers or artists so much as the ability of the man in the street to judge art and literature for himself. In the West, culture tends to be for the few; in the Soviet Union everybody is capable of appreciating it.'

Whether the Soviet public has access to representative art and literature he didn't mention. Of course there are no sexy books, or works of 'bourgeois trashy vulgarity' to choose from, which tends to invalidate the argument. The foreign literature available consists of classics and some new work with the approved point of view; among English translations: Dickens, Shakespeare, Thackeray, Mark Twain, Edgar Allen Poe, Jack London, Dreiser, Hemingway, Galsworthy, Steinbeck, Howard Fast (until present editions sell out), James Aldridge, and a few others; and current Soviet literature is often out of the same sausage machine as the newspapers.

But the Soviet reading public can discriminate, inasmuch as it usually chooses Russian classics far ahead of Soviet socialist realism. New editions of Pushkin, Tolstoy, Gogol, Turgeniev, Lermontov, are sold as fast as they are printed; Gorky and Mayakovsky are the only Soviet writers able to rival their enormous popularity. In general, each example of successful Soviet literature and drama that I saw had (a) an author with genuine revolutionary enthusiasm, and (b) the revolution itself included somewhere in the plot. From then on there are no plots because there are officially no conflicts in Soviet life. Dudintsev, in Not by Bread Alone, presented what I gather from many Russians to be the first book with a genuinely human plot in years. But now the situation, at least temporarily, seems to have reverted away from the 'thaw', and arts are still the handmaidens of politics. They must create positive heroes and postive goals and be moral and instructive, and continually portray what ought to be instead of the worst of what is. Bourgeois 'formalism', the alternative to socialist realism, emphasizes form instead of content, and is likely to generate an 'atmosphere of hopelessness and cynicism', to 'disseminate distrust and pessimism, a sense of submission and hopelessness'. Worthy as the motives behind this policy may be in a growing society (I heard many splendid arguments from non-creators), they succeeded under Stalin in stifling much of Russian drama, literature, and art. What happens next is hard to say, but the ferment that now exists in all creative activity may yet end well.

What is socialist realism? One story I heard was about the famous Soviet general who wanted his portrait painted. Unfortunately, painting the national hero was a definite problem, because he was very ugly—one of his legs was withered, the right side of his face was all mangled and scarred, and he was just four and a half feet tall. An artist was commissioned who thought the only way out was to play down his bad points and make the general pretty; he presented a portrait of a beautiful vision of a general, handsome and straight and tall. The committee which passes on such things was livid. 'You call that socialist realism? What's realistic about that?' and the artist was banned. Another one was commissioned. Taking warning from his predecessor's fate, he produced an exact replica of the general on his canvas. But 'a great socialist man, you paint him like this?' shrieked the committee. 'How can the people see their famous general in all his socialist heroism from this?' and the artist was banned. Then a third was taken on. Terrified, he spent weeks of thought in solving the problem. Eventually he hit on an idea. He painted a picture of the general sitting tall on a horse, with his bad leg on the other side, and showing only the left profile of his face. 'Ah, that is wonderful,' the members of the committee were unanimous. '*That* is socialist realism!'

It is difficult to judge the results of state supervision of the visual arts because Russia has never produced any really major artists. The Tretyakov Gallery in Moscow contains room after room of pre-revolutionary art as appalling as that of the last forty years. But during the Youth Festival I went there with an American artist who said he knew about some good paintings kept out of public view. We wandered through fifty or so rooms of recent work; all of it seemed to us utterly stereotyped and oppressively boring. Finally we came to the door, marked 'no admittance', where the other paintings were. The artist argued with the woman in charge for half an hour, making a strong case for international culture, solidarity, friendship, and anything else he could think of to throw in, and reluctantly, finally, she gave permission. We were shown into a narrow dark room, or hallway, where a curator shone a flashlight for us briefly over hundreds of paintings. Some of them were wonderful, some early out-of-favour work tending towards abstraction. They were all piled on top of each other, stacked up against the wall; the artist with me was so enraged by the lack of care they received that he got into a fight with the curator and we were very soon ushered politely out.

Some of these paintings proved that there had at least been seeds of something once. Their real sin was abstraction. The reasoning behind this resembles that concerning jazz and literature. Art is a reflection of the society which creates it, abstract art is a mirror of the contradictions and confusion of capitalist society, and since the Soviet Union has no such contradictions it cannot produce abstract art. In any case, art must serve the people, who couldn't understand it. But to some extent the people do—or at least they are curious. The nearest thing on view, the room of French Impressionists at the Pushkin Gallery, suppressed until three years ago, is always far more crowded than the others. But on the whole, because Soviet art lowers itself instead of forcing its audience to make some sort of effort for its appreciation, there is little sophistication. And there seemed to be few indications of progress; is there anywhere for this kind of art to go?

After November 7, to celebrate the fortieth anniversary of the revolution, a new exhibition opened in the Manege, originally the tsarist stable and more recently the Kremlin garage. Except for the new soaring-sputnik school, it was the same again—35 million roubles worth of happy reaping peasants, shifted around perhaps, happy healthy steel workers, happy old Lenin, happy happy everybody. There wasn't any critical comment or choice to be made; only a certain amount of confusion because everything seemed exactly alike. A foreign visitor, it was said, having been taken through by his Intourist guide, was asked afterwards for his opinion. 'Mm . . . well, not bad, really,' he answered. 'Isn't it remarkable that one artist can paint so many pictures!'

But the queue outside was constant and long. The Muscovites all wanted to see, and they appeared to enjoy what they did see. To me, at the time, it all seemed like some intricate bluffing game, in which an artist painted what he knew would be approved, it was duly approved by members of a committee who each thought he should like it and that the others liked it, and the people gave a favourable opinion because they assumed it must be good to be there. I think I was wrong, though, because appreciation seemed to be genuine.

Among intellectuals it caused nothing but embarrassment or scorn; they couldn't even mention Soviet art except apologetically. Artists themselves, many of them, ignore it, creating what they want and living a precarious existence because they can't exhibit or sell their work. Or they can paint the occasional picture of Lenin and eat and paint what they want for months on the proceeds. Even so, their problems are enormous: with little leadership or criticism, and no contact with their foreign contemporaries, they proceed blindly with little consciousness of progress or direction. Many writers and poets have the same temporary-pot-boiler approach as the Lenin painters. One of my writer friends, a real America fan and a confirmed 'progressive' (Soviet right-wingers and dissenters call themselves progressive), supported himself by making up articles about the disastrous living conditions of the American proletariat. Actually he and the artists like him are primarily concerned with art and only incidentally with politics, but the second is a direct result of the first. Any government which could stifle what is to them life itself, and encourage bad art and the philistinism which they feel results, is logically no good, they say. They probably wouldn't concern themselves with such problems were they left alone to pursue their decadent philosophy of art for art's sake.

A country whose population values knowledge produces children who desperately want to learn and get the best education possible. Where I went to school, ideas were often something to be ashamed of, and if some had accidentally been absorbed they had to be concealed at all costs. In Russia education is a source of pride, a necessity for all who are capable. Even Shura thought that there was probably more freedom of educational opportunity in the USSR than anywhere else, because there are no economic difficulties—all students receive generous state stipends, with bonuses for good marks. These two factors: desire for education and unlimited opportunity to get it, are what produce the growing number of knowledgeable Soviet generations which the West fears.

The West's perpetual consolation is the theory that the Soviet young, provoked to thought, will use its ability to overthrow the government. I disagree because, from what I saw, I didn't feel that most people, however much their education, want to overthrow anything. But some definitely want to *change* things, and with many students this attitude is a direct result of their compulsory lectures in political economy, when they begin to observe contradictions between what they are taught and what they see. Very many, on the other hand, are not receptive to any such stimulation and never learn to think. There are even more who can think, but arrive at the same conclusions as their teachers. The most extreme are the ones so infected with revolutionary zeal that they often choose their careers simply because of the requirements of the country. Students volunteer to take agriculture or geology or forestry so they can help develop the virgin lands; they get their degrees, then go off by the scores of trainloads, into the wilderness for life.

The Foreign Game

MANY PARTIES WERE GIVEN towards the end of the year. I went to one at an institute with some of the students. Or, more exactly, I didn't *go*, I was *smuggled*. My friends insisted on this sort of business quite often, half through unnecessary fear and half for 'exciting'. The exciting usually overcame the fear, showing how unnecessary it was, because like a perfect murder, it's really not any fun if you have to keep it to yourself.

Elaborate preparations: 'We'll leave our coats in the car, and tell the man at the door that we were just walking around the building so we don't need a pass for you. Whatever we say, you say "*da*". Don't talk!' and so forth.

The doorman was an unsporting type, painfully indifferent to everything about us. That dampened, but didn't daunt, the students, and on we crept, in towards the din, prepared to meet any emergency that might arise in our sinister drama. One of the students aimed a hearty monologue at me and I da-ed back when another of them kicked me for the cue. The fact that we were moving and speaking so peculiarly caused concern, if nothing else, among some members of the crowd, who stopped in their tracks and gaped at us.

Inside a big hall draped with decorations, hundreds of couples waltzed intensely around the floor. Pigtails and frizz—half the girls thick and peasant-like in standard Gum-type clothes and neat braids, the others dressed to kill in foreign-looking ensembles, everything from tailored winter suits to summer evening dresses. A lot of the festival had stayed behind, obviously. Less contrast among the boys, though one or two looked smooth in tapered trousers and silk ties. They were all very very serious, didn't seem to say much to each other or laugh, and maintained a decorous distance between themselves and their partners. Sometimes a couple would break into a few bars of rather sedate jitterbugging, then think better of it. The band, later on, played thunderous rock 'n' roll quite blatantly, but no one danced it.

The conspiracy was revived when the students with me spotted a group of sour-looking individuals standing in one corner. They apparently were very significant, because I was kept carefully away from them, dancing down at the other end of the room. The Komsomol leaders, it was explained later. Every time the music stopped, there was a dizzy switch between my partner and one of the others in our group, who would tear across the room and whirl me away before anyone else could interfere and discover my identity. This continued for a couple of hours; I wasn't once allowed to open my mouth. Feeling immensely proud of their success in keeping me anonymous (but also madly arousing everyone's curiosity), my friends congratulated each other as we left.

When they went back to the institute after the weekend, apparently almost everyone in the place came up to them and asked them where they had found the American girl. They had all known right from the start, because someone there had recognized me from the festival and a few others from a film of it, and the word had gone around. Those who had brought me (though I wasn't me, I was a symbol) had their prestige soar to unprecedented heights, and there were no repercussions, but it didn't prevent them from attempting the deception again the next, and each, time I saw them. Everybody played the foreign game, and no nationality was sacred. It worked both ways: just as I had to be Russian, Russians had to be foreign when necessary.

I first saw how during an evening with two young men I'd met at a party with Sergei. They were even farther gone than *stiliagi*—real 'hooligans' and proud of it. Petya, one of them, had an important father, a minister of the RSFSR, and he had grown up completely irresponsible. The other, Genya, had been orphaned in the early years of the war, and had grown up wild. He was a sort of self-styled Dan'l Boone, and the leader of the two. When they weren't causing some kind of havoc in town, they got their excitement out of such unusual distractions as Siberian bear hunting (Genya had a bearskin rug and a very long, wobbly scar down his chin as trophies), and stealing icons out of old Russian churches. The latter was really to finance the former; icons are worth a fortune to foreign tourists, and a summer icon-hunting excursion to the east or north could keep them in pocket-money for a year.

We were at Genya's place, sitting on the bear—uncomfortable but he insisted—and I answered absurd questions about Elvis Presley and was it true that everyone in America had a swimming pool and a private aeroplane. We weren't getting along too well. At about eleven, Genya produced some vodka, sweet Georgian wine, salami, black bread, pickles, and mineral water. Disgusted with me for shattering some of their illusions, they set to on the vodka with even more of a vengeance than the normal Russian vengeance. I hated neat vodka and it was sacrilege to mix it with anything, and the wine was like syrup. But they were determined that I keep up with them, and got really angry when I quit right at the beginning. I want to go home, please could I go home, I begged. You wait, drink something, they answered. No thank you. Silence from them, and a prolonged session aimed at filling every internal crevice with alcohol. Please can I go home. *Drink* something! I tried, but stopped halfway. Don't you know that in Russia you cannot put a glass down that is half full? You must finish it! What's the matter with you—you don't like our Russian vodka?

And so on, until the bottles were empty. In a fit of remorse, Genya gave me one of his prize icons, a very beautiful one that he'd nearly been caught wrenching from the wall of a Siberian church. That seemed to have been the intention, just as with the bear hunting it was necessary to half kill himself. You couldn't just sneak up on an unsuspecting bear and drill him in the head, there had to be a wrestle with him first, the object being to approach death as nearly as possible yourself before the slaughter.

They were just about past anything, but volunteered nobly to find a taxi for me. We walked down to 'Broadway' (Gorky Street); it was late and we passed no one but a few women clearing away the falling snow, and one couple going home from a restaurant. Petya started singing folksongs in a loud drunken baritone and Genya ran ahead and threw snowballs back at us. Suddenly, a crash, as Genya missed and hit a store window. He and Petya stopped short, looked at each other, then walked on sedately. Petya resumed his song, but softly, and this time I realized it was 'C'est si bon'. People materialized from nowhere and gathered around the smashed window ('C'est si bon, don't look back don't look back . . .' sang Petya) and a night watchman started coming for us. Genya spotted him sideways and began talking to me in conspicuous English. The watchman, who had been striding forward angrily, slowed down when he heard this. He came nearer slowly, swore vaguely and said something else, but his tone indicated that it was only token abuse and he'd be willing to forget the whole thing. Petya started reciting a poem in English—it didn't matter what he said—and the watchman faltered, then turned and walked back. I found a taxi.

I often saw this foreign trick used later, and rarely saw it fail. Foreigners inspired so much awe, as well as contempt, that anyone who could get away with it—who looked remotely foreign and knew one French song or English poem—could always use the pretence to overcome awkward situations. Sometimes the approach was non-comprehension of Russian, although success with this seemed fantastic because there just were no such animals in Moscow in the winter except me. In the summer there are tourists, but most foreigners there permanently or semi-permanently can speak the language, and there aren't too many of them around anyway. The other way was a heavy accent. I was recruited to give lessons.

English was the standard nationality choice. Seventy per cent of all students learn it—and all from a standardized text-book it seemed. Their dialogue was heavily peppered with such phrases as 'so to say', and every 'thank you' got the inevitable reply: 'dawn't myention eet'. The most curious one was the 'maybe yes, maybe no, maybe rain, maybe snow' routine, which could be counted on to appear at least once an hour in any English conversation. They listened to the Voice of America and the BBC for pronunciation practice, and some were so adept at mimicry that they could out-English an Englishman. The BBC reportage, by the way, was much preferred over the Voice—which many felt was nothing but unbelievably naïve propaganda. Both the American and British Russian-language broadcasts were jammed (except for a brief period before Hungary) but most of the English-language programmes got through. Now and then there was selective jamming—I was listening to the BBC news one evening during the Syrian crisis, when suddenly, following the mention of the word 'Syria', the radio started making the most extraordinary exploding noises.

The most usual game time was Saturday night at the restaurants. The 'Restaurant is Closed' signs (which enigmatically meant that the restaurant was open but there were no tables free, or at least not very many tables) came out quite early, but crowds of hopeful couples would congregate near the doors to corner the doorman and try coaxing, or to wait for someone to leave. No one did leave because they were all there for the evening. But someone with a system, if he managed to catch the doorman's eye long enough to gain his ear as well, could mumble something stupid in thick Russian and immediately get ceremoniously swept inside. What the thick Russian consisted of didn't matter, but it was preferable to work in the magic word *delegatsia*. The waiters abased themselves with extremely untypical fast and efficient service, the maitre d'hotel hovered nearby rubbing his hands together, and nothing was too much to ask.

It worked with film tickets too; such a long-term project, unless you knew the game. Then you could go spontaneously, tell the manager that you were a visiting Czechoslovakian, dispense with the queue, and get the best seats in the house.

Then there were the various brushes with authority, such as the shop-window episode or public brawls, or other non-cultured behavior. It worked wonders with traffic violations too. There always seemed to be militiamen waiting at the tops of hills—since passing on a hill was prohibited, Russian drivers would wait for a hill before they passed. Sometimes there wasn't one for miles, and it slowed everything up. When it came, zoom ahead, and there at the top was that old militia-man, waiting to invalidate a third of the licence. The act then: sobstuff in a foreign accent, and everyone nudging me to start making a speech. The militiaman, all charm, would salute and wave us on.

This was all very fine, except that most of the time it could only breed more of the awe and innate distrust of foreigners that were already so acute. I tried to explain, but could never convince, that it was against everyone's interests to keep it up.

And then I had to have a flexible nationality too. To go to someone's house I had to be Russian, for movies and restaurants American (because that was so fantastic even Russians hesitated to use it), for special favours East European, and for places that required me to speak in front of strangers, sound foreign but still be above suspicion, I was a Latvian or a Soviet Eskimo.

The thing that baffled me continually was exactly what I *was* supposed to symbolize. I was working for an official organization, presumably had their approval, and was in no way barred from meeting anyone I wanted. But my Russian friends were convinced that they would be accused of something sinister if they were caught with me as an American, so worked out all these involved situations to disguise it. However—on the one hand there wasn't anything visibly wrong with their seeing me, and on the other, even if there were, those who wanted to know certainly would in any case, and scheming could only make it far worse. But everybody had a well-developed sense of the dramatic, and loved to scheme.

There was absolutely no indication that I was under scrutiny. The only thing that made me wonder once or twice was an extremely handsome, suave, and un-Russian Russian who was sicked on me by the publishing house, ostensibly to discuss work but in fact only to take me to his 'favoreet leetle café' every so often and talk about my views. Which must have confused him quite a lot, but he was a demon for punishment. He was another everything-is-perfect man, but had had enough dealings with sophisticated foreigners to be able to tone down his more obnoxious panegyrics. In the end it turned out that he worked for the Foreign Ministry, which may or may not have had some deep significance. If he really was checking up on me, I could only give the ones who had cast him for the role a hundred marks out of a hundred. But it's just as possible that it was all for his personal amusement.

What about fear, and how much did it still represent? Who were these mysterious people behind it all?

Petya called me the day after the snowball adventure to apologize. He said he had arranged for me to go to see someone who would really interest me, and could I look Russian please and meet him in the city centre at 7. He wouldn't give me any clues about what this third person was, but guaranteed it would be *ochen, ochen interesna.*

The Metropole lobby, 7, Petya. He rushed me outside and down a maze of streets until no one was around. Then he opened a door and pulled me inside. He took a gun out of his coat.

'What are you doing?' Good Lord, what now.

'I wanted to show this to you; don't worry! Look.' He gave it to me and showed me the handle. It had a silver plaque mounted on it with an inscription. Something about it being presented to someone or other for his long years of loyal service for the GPU.

'GPU?'

'Ssh! Yes. Listen. I have this friend—you know about my father, big Soviet man?—well, this friend of my father, who was one of Beria's boys. Of course not any more. He thinks I am good Komsomolitz, very much likes me. He presented this to me. Good? Ha, I think this good one! I hope someday I can use it against him. Nu, so I have told him that I have a friend who is a member of the English Communist Party, who would very like to meet him. You! I had to say this English because his son knows some English. You must say nothing about America! So we will go there now. Come.'

The gun, the GPU, the whole thing left me functioning only just enough to follow. We took the metro, then two buses, then weaved back again in a taxi until I had no idea where we were. Approaching a big building, Petya warned: 'Not a word now, no one must know.'

'But . . .'

'Tsst!' and he carried on the da act with me for the benefit of the people we passed going in.

We were let into a large and comfortable flat, full of over-stuffed furniture and bric-a-brac. A smiling woman, her smiling son, and a jolly old Santa Claus of a man welcomed us and we all sat down. They couldn't have been more pleasant and hospitable. We had tea and all that food again. The son, a husky boy of about thirteen, wearing several badges on his shirt (among them a Komsomol membership badge and a miniature bas-relief portrait of Lenin), tried out his English with some questions about the festival and the English youth movement. I wildly manufactured answers that befitted one of my station. When he had run out of questions, his father began. Chortling and chuckling, he was enjoying this very much. He took large glasses of water from a jug beside him, drank them down and refilled. I kept feeling that there was something wrong with his eyes; they seemed somehow reptilian, calculating, like pinpoints in those masses of beaming flesh. But then I forgot, and we chatted on. Petya, exceptionally pleased with himself, sat on the arm of a chair surveying it all, and looking so much the picture of innocence that it nearly killed me.

After a while the conversation headed towards the rest of the world, trips and holidays. Like any family anywhere, this one wanted to show me a photo album of a tour they had taken of Kazakhstan some years before. They brought it out and turned the pages slowly, relating witty anecdotes around all the pictures. Camels, round tents (*yurts*) made of felt, Mongol, moon-faced nomad herdsmen. Then suddenly there didn't seem to be anything at all left to say, and Petya announced that we had to leave to meet some friends. Kindly and graciously, they thanked him for bringing me and asked me to visit them again.

We walked silently for some distance.

'Did you notice what he was drinking?' Petya said finally. 'Vodka. He likes people to think it is water. You think Genya and I am bad—he never stops, just sits there all day filling his glass. So . . . he can forget, I suppose.'

'Forget what?'

'Forget all the people he has killed! That man is responsible for hundreds, thousands, maybe millions of deaths. Didn't you see his eyes? He is scum!' Petya spat.

'Does he do anything now?'

'No. He cannot. After Beria, they made him go. They shouldn't have been so kind. He was never so kind. He was one of the first people who helped begin the secret police.' He paused for effect. 'And the photographs! Ah, that is *really* interesting.'

'Why?'

'Camels! Pah! That was no holiday. That was a trip to Kazakhstan to find a place for a concentration camp.'

*   *   *

Concentration camps, terror, reptilian eyes, 'black life', 'the tortures and inhumanities of Peter the Great . . .'

'We all have this dream,' Kolya said the next day, 'but we are not confused like you. We have pulled ourselves out of all this, this blackness is *ended*; we know where we have come from and where we are going. Don't forget these things—none of us must ever forget—but see them where they belong.'

I can, more clearly, now. Then, there was still everyone's fear to live with, and mine too. Dream and reality—there was no line dividing them, or separating past from present either, or horror from reason, or melodrama from truth. And some real blackness, that wasn't ended, still haunted me.

Shura's brother Yuri was ignorant of the world outside Russia, but he had the idea that Italy was It, Italy was the ultimate. If he ever was able to leave, he said, he would roar straight off to Italy, lie on top of a mountain in the sun for weeks, perhaps months, and shout and scream and rave anything he wanted. He had planned all the details, and with no provocation regularly bored anyone within reach about it. Naturally, when he played the foreign game, he had no difficulty making a choice of nationality. One of the main things, of course, was to learn Italian. He had regular lessons twice a week, and often when I went to talk to Shura, Yuri would be studying in a corner. He had found Giuseppe to teach him.

Giuseppe was completely *simpatico*. We didn't talk to each other very often, and what we did was in French, but words weren't necessary. His warmth came out and gave everything near him a glow. So did his sadness—just the sight of him made people feel like weeping. He was little and frail, about forty-five, with the most enormous tragic eyes. Sometimes, when he came and left and during breaks in Yuri's lessons, he had tea with us and we talked a little, but I never knew his story until much later when Shura told me. He had to, because it proved his case too well to withhold.

Giuseppe had come to Russia twenty-five years before, an eager young Communist wanting to help the Soviet Union in any way he could. His language was most useful; he did translations and taught a little. When Stalin became his most xenophobic in the 'thirties, Giuseppe was accused of being a spy. They tried to make him confess, and he was systematically tortured. Each of his fingers had been broken and he still bore the marks of it: the knuckles were swollen and distorted like an arthritic's. Whether he did finally 'confess' or not doesn't matter—in those days it was a mere formality, and in any case he was sent to Siberia.

He was one of those who lived through it, and was rehabilitated in the amnesty after Stalin's death. All he wanted then was to go home and begin a new life, without vindictiveness, to forget and start completely over again. Through the years the memory of his home had come back to him with increasing frequency and intensity until now it obsessed him—but his tragedy was that he thought he couldn't go. After repeated requests he had been told that they wouldn't permit his leaving unless he signed a statement saying that he was a Soviet citizen. Since his Italian passport had long ago lapsed, in a way he was, and the government's object presumably was to avoid accusations of brutal treatment to foreign nationals. But Giuseppe couldn't sign, because if he did he believed he would be subject to the same restrictions as a Soviet citizen—who isn't allowed to leave the country. It was an agonizing, futureless predicament. The longer it went on the more futile it seemed, and everyone could almost see Giuseppe gradually losing his hope and his spirit, even though he never failed to be outwardly cheerful. He never wanted others to feel they must share his emotions. He stopped teaching Yuri. A week before I left the country I met him in the metro, head down and walking with weary despair. He brightened when we met —that was the kind of person he was—but after I told him I was leaving he couldn't hide the flash of pain that passed across his face. It was something I could never forget.

A few months after leaving Russia I received a postcard from Giuseppe—postmarked Italy. '*Soyez heureuse et joyeuse!*' he wrote, '*Je suis à Rome!*' There is no explanation of how he did it. But I remember Kolya's words.

8

Leningrad

I WAS TIRED of hearing 'Leningrad, ah beautiful Leningrad . . .' together with the sighs and dreamy looks that invariably accompanied it. It couldn't be as good as all that, but I wanted to *see*, and wasn't able to because of some mangle my identification papers had got themselves into; a month and a half after processing had begun, I still didn't have a document to prove I was me. A passport or equivalent—an identification card with a photograph—was necessary for receiving pay, joining a library, or joining anything, collecting a parcel, and hundreds of other less simple things. The main one, travel. Russians were supposed to carry their passports with them at all times, and didn't travel without them, even from city to city, although it was perfectly possible if one avoided trouble and hotels. As a foreigner, trouble wasn't inconceivable, and a park bench didn't seem appealing in Leningrad in the winter. But one day, hearing my tale of woe, Kolya said he could fix it; he had a friend who would put me up, so all I had to do was stay out of trouble.

'Pretend you're a Finn,' someone suggested. An *Amerikanka* all alone without papers wouldn't go over very big. All right, a Finn. I forgot about that the week before, though, and concentrated on everyone's dreamy dialogue about Leningrad, and the Hermitage, one of the finest art collections there are.

Three people came to see me off on the midnight train,

just as if I were going away for a year instead of a weekend. They brought a bottle of wine and we took turns drinking out of the same glass, which they broke for good luck as the whistle blew. The train was suddenly a squealing mass of people getting out and shouting goodbyes and hugging one another tearfully. Partings of the shortest duration or distance seemed to be as good an excuse as any for great ceremony and profound exhibitions of devotion.

The sexes aren't separated on Russian trains, and in my compartment were three men. They soon caught on that I wasn't a Finn; an English book and a Russian-English dictionary appeared on top when I opened my suitcase. I decided that I wouldn't make a very efficient spy. Two of them were overcome with excitement and curiosity, and we struggled through a conversation about my history and then theirs. The third was a squat, bull-like man whom I imagined to be a loyal, utterly vacant-minded petty bureaucrat. *He* wouldn't have any truck with foreigners, not he—he sat stolidly in a corner gazing out of the window, though there was nothing to see, and kept asking for tea to drink with a huge parcel of *pirozhki*, with which he kept stuffing himself, it seemed to me, all the way to Leningrad. In the end he let himself go to the point where he shot fierce glances at us now and then, but he never entered into the conversation.

Of my two friends, one was a tall, spare, laughing man with a mouthful of stainless steel teeth. He was a worker on his way to see his brother in Leningrad, and seemed to feel that the whole train ride, and his holiday, in fact all of life, was a glorious stroke of luck.

The other was an intellectual, perhaps an inventor like Lopatkin, I thought. He had nothing with him but a case full of books and papers, and didn't seem the least concerned with clothes or food or any of the things that usually pre-occupy man. He kept saying 'I love you, I love you. One two three four', which was his total English vocabulary and the source of much pride. He jumped up and down in his seat agitatedly every time we failed to understand each other, and was terribly upset that he hadn't brought along his daughter, who was learning English in school, to find out everything about me and my world. He knew German, but had even less success with that than me with my French, so we struggled along in Russian.

Before I went to bed I sat by the window and watched darkened Russia speed by. Except from the stars there was no light by which to see what we passed, but the shining trunks of white birches gave everything a pale luminosity. Ta-pocketa-pocketa-pocketa, 300 miles. It was the same sort of train as the trans-Siberian, and rather like the one that had been our base for six weeks of travel around China, so I felt almost as if I'd come home. There was the same wood fire at the end of the corridor where the attendant heated a huge samovar for tea, and the tea itself, strong and hot in glasses with metal holders, as special to Russian railways as a different kind is to British railways. The ridiculous water faucet in the lavatory still shot water up, down and sideways, drenching the whole room; the mattresses were still six inches too short for the beds and a foot shorter than any ordinary-sized person; the radio in each compartment shrilled the same folk music and of course the knob to turn it off, like all the other knobs in all the other trains, had mysteriously disappeared. But I slept better than I had in months, with that familiar rattling and lurching.

When I woke up there was light to see by, infinite and grey, distended over horizontal nothingness. We passed a few of those incredibly isolated and colourless villages that spread their identical selves across the 4,000 miles of Russia that I had seen; and occasionally interrupted the work of women in the inevitable high felt boots, shawls, and grey padded jackets above flimsy skirts, who were fixing a section of track. They stopped as we passed and leaned on their shovels and picks, breathing out clouds of warm white air and gazing at us expressionlessly. Then suddenly there was Leningrad, springing up abruptly like all the other cities, with little suburban transition from wilderness to civilization.

Kolya's friend was to recognize me by a yellow scarf, but just as the train was pulling in I couldn't find it. I had no idea how I would know him, and there were hundreds of people on the train, so I got into a panic and dumped out my suitcase, searched on the shelves and luggage rack, and was beginning to get mildly hysterical when my intellectual friend came in, saw my distress and consoled: 'I love you, I love you!' When I'd conveyed what was the matter, he helped look and in the end crawled under the bunk. 'One . . .' his voice echoed out, '. . . two . . . three . . . FOUR!' he waved the scarf out behind him. 'I LOVE YOU!' he jumped up.

So Misha Pavlovich Lomov found me. He looked, of all things, rather American. The crew-cut did it, and he had finer bones than most Slavs, but everything about him seemed to suggest the clean-cut look of an Ivy League undergraduate. When I told him, he wasn't at all sure whether to consider it a compliment or base slander, or maybe he had no feelings about it at all. His whole attitude was unemotional. It was odd being accepted as a human being for once instead of a supernatural Marsman.

His parents' car, a Pobeda, was outside in the square. As we approached it, so did two couples, a young boy, and a babushka—wanting lifts. Three of them going our way clambered in the back. Leningrad is big, Misha explained, the metro still small, and taxis difficult. We drove down the Nevsky Prospect, through the city and over the river. And it really was as good as all that. Each building is related to the others and the whole is a masterpiece of harmony. Little of it has changed; palaces have become apartment houses or clubs, clinics, ministries, but they still look like palaces. Every one is pastel stucco, first pink, then yellow, grey, peach, blue, green, with white columns and sculpted decoration. Monuments and statues in each square, a gold spire, a bright dome, and through it all rivers and canals and trees. The 'Window into Europe' seemed in fact far more Western than Moscow, in spirit as well as location.

We stopped at the Lomovs' flat to drop off my things. It

was a surprise—decorated with a simplicity that I'd never seen before in a country of things heavy, ornate, and fringed. Where? How? They had made all the furniture themselves, Misha said, casually, as if nothing could be more natural. Who were these remarkable people? But he wouldn't talk about himself, except to tell me what I already knew, that he was a journalist and his parents professors, one of biology and the other of architecture. He was pleasant, he was relaxed, he was fine, but the feeling persisted that something wasn't real.

That afternoon we walked through miles of the Hermitage. The building itself is beautiful, the art supreme, and in quantity too much to see even a tenth of it at once. Misha knew every corner of every room, and got us through as much as he could with a professional running commentary. He had been saving up his Rembrandts, his favourites, and at last we got there. At last, also, his exterior cracked.

'I have come to this room ever since I was very little.' He looked at a portrait of an old woman and seemed lost in it. 'That light. . . there is nothing like that anywhere. Whenever anything is wrong and I am sad . . .'

In a split second he stopped himself, and guided me on, upstairs to the French Impressionists. There were some superb Van Goghs, Cézannes, Matisses, Gauguins, that I hadn't known existed. He looked at each one as I did, as though he'd never seen it before.

Hours and miles later, I asked for a pause and a cigarette. There is nowhere here where one is permitted to smoke, he said, but maybe if we went out to the stairway no one would catch us. We did, and he gave me a *papirosa*. A minute later, a passing man saw us smoking, stopped, and pulled out his own cigarettes. Five minutes later you couldn't see the stairs for the people and the smoke.

Misha asked me about other art I had seen in the Soviet Union, and I barged right in, with my usual diplomatic genius, about the Tretyakov and the hidden paintings. His reaction was absolutely nil; he just stood there. All at once, with an almost perceptible click, he seemed to make up his mind—

to expose his other self, the real one. People had told me about the Russian schizophrenia, and it had happened, but this was the first time I saw the transition.

'There are worse things,' he said. 'There is other painting and sculpture that we took from the Germans in the war. No one knows about it. They're hidden away now while Soviet artists make copies. Perhaps they will give them back then, but it may be a very long time, and no one knows where they are.' He had a friend who had seen them, he said, an artist who had somehow got into the vaults. He knew a number of artists, and offered to arrange a meeting.

'They might interest you—you wouldn't see any of their work anywhere else. Out of favour—some of it like the Western, abstract and so on. You understand about our art situation, but there is a lot more than what is in museums. We aren't as bad as perhaps you think; there are many who paint as they feel but of course can never show any of their work to anybody. They would be happy to meet you. They are in a . . . an isolation, so they are not what they could be. Well, we will visit one of them tomorrow, and you'll see yourself.'

He crushed his cigarette and led me back through the Rembrandts, then we left for home, both much happier. Misha said that even though I was a useless decadent bourgeois, I might still go down in Soviet history as the founder of smoking in the Hermitage. Heroine of Socialist Smoking.

At dinner Mr Lomov was extravagantly gay and cheerful. He immediately started talking about a trip he had taken to London once as a member of a scientific delegation. His English vocabulary was only slightly less restricted than that of the man on the train, but now and then he remembered a word and started constructing sentences, partly German, around it. His good spirits seemed to be mainly to compensate for his wife, who was polite but grim. She didn't look very happy about my being there. Misha didn't say anything.

After an interminable series of courses the meal was over, and Misha's parents left the kitchen.

'I'm very sorry.' He sighed thoughtfully. 'I didn't think it would be this way. My mother is afraid, she worries all the time, and my father decided that it would be good if you came and she could see how things have changed. She lives a long way behind. Her brother was sent away, and she was very fond of him—now she is sure that we will be too. She has an important job, and she thinks she would be accused of giving you information.'

'But if she wanted to give me information she wouldn't have me *stay* here. I mean it wouldn't be so obvious—how could anyone suspect her?'

'They wouldn't, but there was a time when things happened with far less reason than that. Her brother, and all her other memories.'

'What happened to her brother?'

'I never met him. He was very young, their parents were dead and he was everything to her. He had a girl friend. I don't know what happened, but he jilted her I think. She wrote a letter to the secret police and told them that he was plotting to overthrow the government—he was arrested. He was nineteen years in a camp, then he died. He was innocent of course, he had much faith, as my mother has too—but that didn't prevent anything. So you see.'

'Maybe it would be better if I didn't stay here.'

'No. Why? Don't talk about it.'

We washed the dishes and made coffee. Misha took two cups out for his parents.

'She is feeling better now,' he said as he sat down again. 'It is very important that you stay here, I'm sorry it is like this, but don't feel bad about it. It will help. Even me.'

'You?'

'It is very strange, all of this. I was worried too—a little because of everything my mother has said. She never stopped, all this week, more and more, and I suppose it was that that did it to me too. Today when I met you at the station . . . well, I don't know, I thought of all kinds of things. I brought a friend with me to see if you were followed. He was behind us, and if anyone was with you he was going to walk past and whistle—that French song, *Les Feuilles Mortes*. But it's all right. *Everything* will be all right.' He didn't sound very convinced.

The next freezing afternoon Misha took me to see his friend the artist. As we walked I asked him about his work. He knew nothing about the Western press and assumed that newspapers everywhere were the same, except that Western ones probably lied more and they were too sensational. Journalism wasn't his main enthusiasm anyway, he said. He did it because he had to do something, and because he wanted to write.

'Poetry is my heart, my soul, my everything!' he spoke again as he had in the Rembrandt room.

'Has any of it been published?'

'No, no it hasn't. Perhaps some day—perhaps soon. It is different, I don't think it could be approved now. Too much . . . pessimism, not socialist realism. Like my friend's paintings. I cannot translate my work to you well enough, but his you can see. Here we are.'

We had been passing many old and beautiful buildings, and had come to a slightly frayed but gorgeous pink palace. Inside, it bore little resemblance to anything palatial: the paint and plaster hadn't been renewed and the floor was full of holes. Now and then a huge, once-gilt door, a moulding, a peeling fresco, served as reminders of its origins. We walked through long corridors which got narrower as we went, and Misha said it was the old servants' quarters. Every inch of floor had been converted into living space. Boris, the artist, lived with his wife and and baby in part of a hallway that had been blocked off at both ends and chopped into rooms. The front door opened into the kitchen which was shared by two families living on either side of it.

Boris's piece of hall was furnished poorly and filled with canvases and paints. Its artistic disadvantages were great— there was only one tiny window with a view of a brick wall, and so little space that it seemed impossible for three people to live and one to paint there. But Sonya, his wife, went out all day, because she earned their living as well as taking up too much room. The baby was in a crèche.

Boris was a wildly radiant little man with a shiny face, stubby nose, and the very sweet smell of Russian barbershop hair tonic. To think! Meeting someone who had seen the art of Europe and America! He jumped around all over what space there was, like an especially enthusiastic puppy. I looked at the painting he was working on. It was slightly abstract, two people looking distantly and hopelessly out across a river. He flew through the other paintings against the wall, terribly anxious for my approval and scattering canvases in every direction. When they were distributed around the room he stood in the middle, folded his arms, and looked at me expectantly. Misha was very excited. Ah, *khorosho, ochen khorosho*—good, very good—he commented on some of them. I didn't know what to say and couldn't really help at all; I wished everybody didn't automatically expect me to be a genius, or I wished I were a genius so they could all be happy. He was very talented, though, anyone could see that. He had dabbled in all extremes of abstraction, but in a way it seemed someone's dream of abstract art—someone who didn't understand it or feel it but painted what he did out of a general spirit of protest. He was essentially a realist, and his best pictures were very real, and very tragic. A sketch of a starving woman, with a look of bleak horror on her face. Another of bent, spiritless people walking down a road. Some of his work was not just depressing, but morbid, and seemed utterly incongruous coming from such a happy-go-lucky creature.

He was still waiting for my opinion, and looked as though it would mean a great deal to him. I made every comment I could, and admired some of his portraits. He leaped around rapturously, seized Misha's hands and danced up and down. We talked about Western art until I ran out. Then 'Come on, let's go for a walk!' Boris pounced up and landed approximately on the bed, grabbed a coat and whooshed us out the door.

He lived next to the Neva, and we walked along the embankment for a few hundred yards. The river and sky were pale grey and very still, but on each bank the pastel palaces reflected colour into the water. They looked like tinted ice cubes. Boris made me feel practically senile; he bounced along and whistled, waving his hand at all around us and pausing now and then to comment on his city. 'My beauty, my wonder . . .' He asked me if I noticed how truly remarkable Leningrad was, how beautiful, how alive, how cultured, how indeed *perfect* it was. 'Moscow? Oof!' He jolted along for a while, whistling again, then suddenly screeched to a stop.

'Let's take her to see Peter's babies!' he said to Misha, who shrugged vague agreement. We came to an archaeological museum and inside Boris went off somewhere. He came back with a curator, who led us through twisting corridors and halls full of stuffed Eskimos and things, unlocking doors and switching on lights as we went. 'Peter's babies' we came to at last. It was a hall full of two-headed babies, four-legged babies, one-eyed Cyclops babies, one-legged mermaid babies, every conceivable variation on the theme, pasty greenish-white and pickled in bottles. And they were born 250 years ago— Peter was Peter the Great: a hobby of his. Misha began to look bored, but Boris sprang blithely through, laughing and pointing with glee. 'The second head is rather an improvement on the first, don't you think?' 'Look at the blue of its eye!'

'This is what he does with his time,' mumbled Misha.

Halfway around I'd had enough, and Boris was persuaded to leave but he wouldn't speak to me after that. His spirits returned to him only after we had crossed the river and turned into the Nevsky Prospect. The street was crowded with shivering shoppers, and Boris, expressing his disgust with people in general, suggested we get off the street and have some ice cream. What a wonderful idea, I muttered through chattering teeth to Misha, who didn't see my point. A *morozhenoye* café was nearby, and at least it would be warm, my consolation. It was, warm and comfortable and nice, in fact perfect, especially since it was early and the band wasn't playing. Boris and Misha had colossal dishes of pink, beige, green and white ice cream, and started an involved Russian discussion with the waitress, whom Boris seemed to know. He was still cross with me for my lack of appreciation of his babies, and only talked to me, obliquely, when absolutely necessary.

There were all kinds of people in the café for me to look at. A very handsome young Komsomolitz and a beautiful scrubbed and pigtailed Komsomolka, of maybe seventeen, were sitting at the next table gazing at each other blissfully. They didn't say a word and had forgotten about their ice cream. Three matronly shoppers, very fat, spooned theirs into their mouths, their arms going up down up down, regularly and then faster, as if they were having a race; they weren't talking either. A high-pitched giggle behind me—a girl in a tight kelly green sweater and frizzy hair, who could conceivably have been pretty but had neither the ability nor material for success. She was sitting with a middle-aged gold-toothed man in a baggy suit. I stared too long; they looked up and, breaking off their conversation, stared long and coldly back.

'A prostitute,' said Boris, watching too. His waitress had gone off in a huff about something. 'Another one over there, but different.' Over there was a girl rather like a *stiliagi's* girl-friend, quite attractive. 'Free. This one here is a pay one.' There aren't brothels, he said, and not many professionals, because their market is usurped by the free ones.

We sat looking at them; then suddenly Boris leaned across the table, looked at me gravely, and asked, 'What do you do for sex?'

This took a minute. 'Who, me? Or Americans?'

'Oh, you know. In *general.*'

'The same as you, I guess.'

'Ah, but there are difficulties sometimes here, very serious difficulties, in a way it is probably not for you over there.

Mmm . . .' he glanced over his shoulder at the waitress. I looked at Misha; he smiled and nodded.

'Yes, difficulties . . .' Boris turned back and popped his chin in his hands. 'Space, is what I mean. And neighbours—such neighbours! Of course, Sonya and I—we understand each other, and so on, you know. But neighbours! And with my painting, I am in no position to . . . Well, and then of course there are some families who are very considerate, they see how things are, and they go out, leave their daughters, their sons. But then, there are others, altogether different, the other side of things altogether. They live in some past age.'

He stared into space. 'Nu, all there is—art. But what is there for me? This dreadful work they do, am I to sell myself? Hm! What time is it? Oh, I am late—I must go now.' He jumped up and inside ten seconds had disappeared.

Misha and I sat there for a minute. Eventually: 'He couldn't pay the bill. He always has to go through this! I'm sorry for my friend, he is very excitable. And strange. Too many things have gone wrong for him—he has had a very difficult time. His grandfather was a noble, for one thing, and that was all very unfortunate. It was hard for him. And Boris —went nearly mad during the war years, the blockade, but it is better now.'

The blockade again. The blockade was a subject always mentioned but never detailed. It had so many associations and emotional memories to those who had been through it that I felt I was inflicting unnecessary cruelty every time I asked to hear the story. At the beginning I learned that Kolya, and many others, couldn't talk about it at all; it was still too close, too full of meaning for them all. I asked again now, I had to, and Misha agreed to tell me. 'It is an awful story, but a great one too, and it is important for you to know.'

Almost every family in Russia, he began, had lost someone, at least one person, in the 'Great Patriotic War' (fifteen million died in all), but the people of Leningrad had lost everything. More than half a million people starved to death. At the beginning the food supplies, instead of being distributed throughout the city, had been concentrated in one place, and that had been bombed. Then, for 900 days, from August 1941 until January 1944, the Germans surrounded the city. The first five months were the worst: Leningrad was almost entirely cut off from the 'mainland' and no supplies could come in. There was nothing to eat, no fuel, electricity, transportation, sewage, water, and the city was ceaselessly shelled besides.

'But there was the *very* greatest self-sacrifice and bravery. From the beginning the people knew that the Germans would not take our city. Everyone went out to fight, young children, grandparents, and all who could walk, helped to build trenches and fortifications. And then life went on, as much as it could. People went to work, children to school, even though they had to walk sometimes a very long way and there was almost no heat. They felt they had to go. The ones who stayed at home had already lost their spirit, and they died there. Thousands of them daily, that way, of hunger and exhaustion. And many times their families were so hungry that they hid the bodies until the end of the month so they could use the ration cards of the dead. It was odd the way people knew they were going to die . . . They would tell you one day—"Now there has been enough for me, and tomorrow will be the end." They never complained or begged or stole food, they just knew, and they didn't want to make it worse for the others. They were—such courage!

'It was terribly cold during that winter, that was one of the biggest battles. We—every family—moved into one room and tried to have a small fire. We burned all of the furniture. What we have now we made after it was all over. And then we had to burn all of our books, and finally there was nothing, and we slept all three together to keep ourselves warm. Then the people who lived in the outer city were moved to the centre, and we had their houses for fuel. Each block and organization was assigned a house, and every morning the ones who could walk would go out and bring back wood for their fires. But sometimes they weren't strong enough . . .

'We had only 125 grams of black bread each day during the worst times. Sometimes there was a little gruel or grain soup. But the water—there was none except from the river, and some died from not boiling their water enough. Because the Neva had to be our sewer too; each morning we brought out pails to throw everything in, when we could. Food—people ate anything during the famine, it was terrible. They ate glue from the furniture, machine oil, anything. They scratched up the dirt from the bombed place where the food had been stored, and made soup, because it was sweet from the sugar that had been there. All the dogs and cats were gone soon. I remember one family who had a dog—they couldn't feed it and it starved to death in the first weeks. Later after three months they dug up its body and ate it. Oh, such times! The people like skeletons, and walking along the street in a trance, and if they bumped into each other and fell they just picked themselves up and went on. No words. Words took too much strength. And all the time there were shells lobbing in over our heads—the Germans were only two miles outside. That noise, all the time. The shells landed in the middle of groups of people and took them all. But after the first shell they knew what to do, and they moved under cover if they could. Incendiary shells too—and since all the water-pipes were frozen, there was only snow to put out the fires. The Germans set fire to everything, and as the armies came nearer there were fires all around us. At night you could look out, in any direction, and there were the glows. But no one gave up!'

Misha had lost sixty pounds, but somehow stayed stronger than most, and volunteered for the hardest labour to get extra rations for his family. Most of the work had been clearing away bodies—there were piles of bodies in all the streets for weeks and no one bothered about them. He remembered one exhausting, very cold day, when he and a group of women (on the whole women were stronger, but they stopped menstruating) were heaving bodies into open sleighs, bringing them to the outskirts and burying them in a mass grave. They had nearly got the job completed when it began to get dark, and everyone was too tired to go on, so they left the grave half uncovered. The next morning when they came back, pieces had been cut from the bodies.

'I was very proud of my parents; they kept me going. They are professors, and valuable, so they could have been evacuated. They refused, they wanted to fight the fight of Leningrad. They helped keep all of our spirits up—all our friends, and I—I think I should have given up without them.'

A few planes got in and out, but there was never anything like a big air lift in the Berlin sense. It was too dangerous. And the planes had to be used mainly for military purposes— a whole front had to be kept supplied. It wasn't until the German bulge along the south of Lake Ladoga was flattened out by the Russian counter-offensive in December 1941 that the Russians were able to use the inland sea as a supply route. When the lake froze over a truck convoy system was organized across the ice from a railhead on the south-east end of the lake to one on the south-west lying just north-east of the city. From that February the ice road went into use in winter, and in the summer some supplies could come across by boat. Rations were increased, but there was still very little. And so life continued as normally as possible, until the blockade was finally smashed in the fighting in January 1944.

Misha sat quietly. Then he sighed and went on, 'All of this was so horrible, yet I can feel all right about it now, and proud. One thing only is the worst for me to remember. I don't know why, but . . . It was in the famine winter, when I was doing that work. I was assigned to go to the Writer's Union. This was awful for me somehow—I had many friends there and I couldn't bring myself to see them the way they were, I hadn't gone there. Then I had to, and when I arrived I saw bodies in every room, they had been there for three weeks, some of them. I met some friends, and I could hardly recognize them at all, they were just lying down to die or they had gone half mad. The intellectuals all went like that, they were the first—their minds weeks before their bodies. Well, I had to begin. I went up to the top, and opened all the doors on the way so that I wouldn't have to stop when I came down. I found five people dead, and I took two, one with each arm. One of them was a friend. And I dragged them down, they were frozen, and the noise . . . I remember. When I got to the first floor, the door was closed and I cursed, it was all so bad. I pushed it and finally it opened, and on the other side there was a woman, so thin, leaning on the door. She looked at me with no expression, then she noticed the bodies. "Who's that?" she said. Then she saw the faces. "Oh, it's my husband." And she just walked out, not looking back. I remember her face . . .

'Well, it doesn't matter,' he said disconnectedly after a long silence. 'It is important for you to see, a little. You cannot imagine what human degradation is. But the Germans didn't get in. They didn't get in. The spirit of this Leningrad, the people of Leningrad—it would have been different anywhere else. We worked and existed, and we kept them out. Bravery! Such bravery I could tell you about! And the pride, now! The people who lived through this—perhaps you can recognize them, one can, because they have scars, and they are old. I was never a child. But we are proud! You see how many things there are that others could never understand, the Americans for instance—about suffering and real heroism. We know what it is, we know war; you don't. I am not blaming you, of course; America did a good job, and America was lucky—but you don't understand really even that. If only you did, perhaps only a little, you would see that *there must never be another war*. We will not have one anyway. We have suffered too much for us even to think of such a thing. We only worry about your Dulles, and some of the others—what they might do because they do not understand.'

He sat, preoccupied, playing with a spoon in his empty ice-cream dish. The he smiled, and looked at me. 'It's funny . . . how much I love my country and my city. I am not sure I ever really knew how much until this moment.' He smiled again, embarrassed now, then stood up suddenly. 'Nu, domoi —let's go home.'

'To Moscow! To Moscow!'

DINNER WAS TENSE. Mrs Lomova appeared to be in a real state of nerves, and no one was trying very hard any more to ignore it. The result of a family conference afterwards was that it would be best if I left tomorrow. Misha, who told me about it, said that she had spoken to a colleague that day who had reinforced her fear of me and the consequences of me, and that now she was near collapse and wouldn't listen to anybody. He offered to find me a place with one of his friends, but I couldn't inflict myself on anyone else. We went out dejectedly after supper to the ballet.

Tickets were as much of a problem as in Moscow. The day before we had plotted, and Misha thought of a plan. He launched me alone into the Astoria, the big Intourist hotel, with instructions that I was to speak only the very best American, look important, and march up to the ticket desk with a story about visiting delegations and wonderful Leningrad and wonderful Astoria, etc etc. It all went fine until they asked me which room I was in so they could deliver the tickets there. I gave a wild guess at a likely hotel room number, and 'please don't bother, I'll collect them myself tomorrow'. It worked.

The only thing was, that I hadn't done too well on my selection. *Spartacus* was what I was longing to see, Khachaturian's new ballet not yet produced in Moscow and causing a stir because of its departure from strict conventional techniques. It wasn't on, so I settled for tickets to a jubilee performance celebrating thirty-five years of a ballerina's career, a show of extracts from three different ballets.

Her principal choice, *Native Fields,* was an Experience. I couldn't do it justice. The scene was a brand-new concrete dam, with a river embankment in the foreground. The whole stage was filled with fluttering red flags—presumably it was dam-opening day, and the populace was celebrating. Some men in wide-trousered (very loyal) Soviet suits congratulated one another. All but one left and he and a girl did a romantic *pas de deux:* two figures in Soviet drapery dancing classical steps, intertwining the ultimate in bad taste with the extreme in beauty.

The multitudes marched on to cheer the people's dam, all dressed as the others—more of the same men's suiting, and the corps de ballet in limp dresses dyed colours exclusively Soviet. They paraded around, joined now by a brass band, all simply oozing the solid strength and collective power always emphasized in their art. At any single moment, as a matter of fact, the scene could have been transferred to canvas and been easily worthy of a place of honour in the Tretyakov. The band played, men made pantomime speeches. A blast of exultant trumpets, heralding the entrance of a procession of strong young men carrying enormous red banners, dancing lightly and expertly around waving them, plus some final mutual congratulating and cheering, added up to a finale of unequalled horror.

I felt as if something sacred had been desecrated. Socialist realism—invading the ballet yet. Misha was in a bad state too; he assured me that he had never seen it before, though, and that it wasn't typical. The audience agreed. For the first time I saw empty seats at a ballet and no more than two curtain calls. Little applause even for the retiring ballerina, and her special fans were there.

*　　　*　　　*

Somehow or other Misha got out of work the next day, and we planned to go to the Hermitage again and do some shopping before I left. I hadn't seen his parents again—they had been asleep when we came home the night before and had already gone to work that morning.

'First we must go to the station and get your ticket.' We went to my room to get my bag. He asked me if it locked and I told him I'd lost the key.

'Is there anything important in it? We will have to leave it in the luggage room at the station.'

'No. A few notes. Does it matter?'

'What notes?'

'My notebooks about Moscow, a few books and things.'

'Well, it might be better to be sure. Can we carry the note-books with us?'

'Oh Misha honestly. No. They're too big.'

'Well, let's see. Open the bag, will you?'

He looked at my slapdash packing job as if he were mem-orizing it. Then he took a hair from the sleeve of my coat and put it through the pages of a book, and shut the suitcase again. This 1984 touch gave me the shudders—it seemed worse than everything else put together. But he hesitated.

'Come on, sit down now for a minute,' he said.

'What for? Let's go.'

'Russian custom. Before a journey everyone must sit quietly for a little time. You don't know this? Another one is that if you forget something you must never go back for it. So you must remember everything now.'

I went for that first Russian custom. It made me remember a pair of stockings, my toothbrush and a book. After these had been collected, packed, rememorized, and we'd sat ponder-ing it all again, we were finally off.

Two lucky tickets for us on the bus to the station. 'Ah, we will be ended right away!' Misha beamed. I didn't find out what he meant until much later, after permanent disillusion-ment had set in over the lucky ticket theory. Much later was that night, after a whole day at the station, unsuccessful at that, and all because I didn't have my passport. Not that identification is necessary for train tickets, but I could have had privileged treatment if I had been able to prove my foreignness. I was all for any privileges going at that stage, considering how little time there was to waste, but they wouldn't take my word for it, and for once the game didn't work. Or it worked in reverse, and they simply wouldn't believe that I wasn't Russian. It was like that children's book about *The Bear that Wasn't*—'You're not a bear,' they all said to the bear, 'You're just a silly man in a fur coat who forgot to shave.' Misha was furious that I hadn't *any* papers, but to him, this alternative, fascinating way to buy a train ticket was hardly worthy of remark. It seemed like Standard Operating Procedure to have to go through it all, and for once their inefficiency was not amusing.

We stood in a shiny, marble, chandeliered hall with about twenty ticket windows down either side and plenty of space in the middle for queues, but nowhere to sit. Scores of people waited at each window, most lines remaining so stationary that the queuers nearly grew roots. Everyone had a sort of glazed expression on his face, as if he'd been waiting for weeks, he'd forgotten why, but he'd lost all desire to go away. Some of them had given up, or perhaps had been waiting for so long that they had eventually collapsed—there were peasants asleep on their bundles all around the walls. Misha started getting the shakes because he was certain that some of them weren't peasants at all, they were secret police in disguise, and if they found out about me they might follow him. *Rule*: there were always MVD men in railway stations. So again, I wasn't permitted to speak. As usual, people kept asking me questions—do I really have that kind of face?—and I had to gesture and point and mumble until they got the idea, which ever one they wanted, that I was either feeble-minded or dumb.

We went from queue to queue, and as each one gradually, almost imperceptibly moved forward and we neared the window, we felt that this was it, at last we would be able to buy a ticket to Moscow and get out of here. Then we reached our destination, and were told either that they didn't know anything, or it was impossible, or it was the wrong window. Moscow was a dream, and I was one of the three sisters. It was a conspiracy, I told Misha, and the hell with them, I'll walk. No, he answered patiently, we would try that window over there this time, that's the one, calm, calm.

At lunch we had someone save our place, and Misha bought me some champagne to cheer me up. It helped, and back we went with hope in our hearts, prepared for anything, ready to win through whatever the odds, to find our friend who was saving our place just where we had left him. The woman at the window had gone to lunch too. We stood, on and on. A peasant in the next line, who had been steadily drinking vodka from a bottle in his pocket, began to get rowdy. He started chanting like a Russian Orthodox priest, but louder and louder and louder until he was finally escorted out the door, with no ticket but a good deal happier than any of us. The woman at the window came back almost an hour and a half later. Aha! But after saying something to the first person in line she shut the window again. 'She says it's impossible,' the word finally reached me. Exactly *what* was impossible continued to evade me until late in the evening, when some solid information was supplied: there were no tickets. No one went away after this announcement, however, which I decided lent definite credence to the root theory. I was getting a little too punch-drunk even to go through the motions of getting Misha out of other people's earshot to ask him why we didn't go away; I just sort of stood there and swayed. It appeared, I found out later, that we were waiting for someone to return a ticket. So were the eighteen people in front of us. Heaven knows what the people in the twenty or thirty other queues were waiting for.

No one did return a ticket, and after a further incalculable space of time Misha led me away. He was despairing: what were we to do? We sat in the snow on a low wall outside while he pondered. I couldn't go back to his house, he insisted, his mother would go to pieces. It was night, and cold. He asked me if I'd like to take a ride on the metro while he figured out a solution. The Leningrad metro then had only seven stations, which didn't go anywhere much, so it was empty. We rode to the end of the line and back three times. Eventually Misha thought of a plan, the first part of which involved going back to the train station. I just didn't care anymore, so I followed meekly. He went to one of our windows and brought a ticket. It was for the next night—no trouble, then, if you organize yourself a day in advance. Then he made a phone call, pulled me outside again, and hailed a taxi.

10

Elenagorsk

'I HAVE TELEPHONED to Boris,' Misha explained. Boris and Sonya were going to leave their baby with its *babushka* and meet us somewhere, then we were going somewhere else, and finally back to Boris's place. It made Misha very excited, whatever it was, and he said he was glad I wasn't leaving that night and we would have a *wonderful* time. He became rather manic in his efforts to cheer me up, but it didn't take long— there was going to be a surprise!

At eight-thirty Boris and Sonya met us in a dingy workers' café, where the food was cheap, the tablecloths grimy, the air fetid, and the general atmosphere much like any greasy spoon. Half the buxom waitresses looked like lady wrestlers, the other half like aged prostitutes. After a snack we set off down the street, Misha looking behind furtively to see if we were being followed. He had automatically registered all the faces in the café. At a nearby corner we boarded a bus, which went over the Neva and out of Leningrad, through snow-and-stars countryside. We sang and laughed, and even Boris behaved like a dream, temporarily anyway. He seemed like the original wholesome Soviet kid. Sonya sat quietly by a window and looked out at the snowy darkness, at times turning to gaze and beam at her husband. She was an extremely pretty girl; I recognized her from some of Boris's paintings. She knew no English, so we spoke bits of Russian and French together, and the conversation switched back and forth in all three languages.

On we rode until the bus was empty except for us and the conductor, a young girl who sat with us and sang along too. After an hour or more we got out. We were deep in the country: dazzling new snow and pines and breathless stillness, and a few timber cottages. Misha still wouldn't say where we were, but now he led us down a long deep-snowy road. At the end was water, and nothing.

'That . . .' Misha pointed across dramatically, 'is Finland.'

We stood there for some time, and the three of them, who had probably never been nearer than that to a foreign country, looked, spellbound, across the black space.

With forced cheerfulness, Sonya took charge and led us away. Considering the effect Finland had had on them, I didn't think too much of Misha's idea, but then it turned out that our real destination was the restaurant of a country hotel nearby. It was filled with raucous peasants, most of them local farmers and caretakers of the *dachas* in the area. We were in a village named Elenagorsk, Misha told me, a vacation resort for Leningrad, with the hotel and a few settlements of cottages. The rich Leningraders who owned *dachas* rarely came out in winter except for occasional weekend ski-ing, so the caretakers enjoyed six months of almost solid alcoholic haze. Not that their condition was exactly hazy just then: a party of men in rough clothes were racketing through their fifth or seventh vodka bottle in a corner, huddling together for a joke then hooting and guffawing apart. Another man had brought his wife along, and they were having a fight. As the curses grew in volume and imagination, the husband began slugging his wife to add emphasis to his. Finally she cracked him on the head with a bottle and he fell over backwards; she became hysterical and shrieked at him, the waiter, the men hooting behind her, the bottle that had done the damage, and the world in general, until her husband picked himself up and she noticed his bloody nose. Suddenly contrite, she dabbed at his face and cooed softly. They had a tearful reconciliation and left, leaning on each other for support.

We had some more champagne. Boris thought the scene was terrible, just too bad. No culture, these people, he kept mumbling. In Siberia it's much worse though, he said—they drank raw alcohol or eau-de-Cologne. 'Ookh, it's the breeding in this country, simply disgusting.' His wife soothed him down a little, but he wanted to leave. Misha paid the bill and we walked outside.

We found a little waterfall nearby among some birch trees, and stood on a bridge above it looking at the snow and icicles. The air was very still, and didn't seem so cold. The only sound was the soft tinkling of the water below us. No one spoke for a long time. The scene inspired Boris; he wanted to stay till morning and draw this by daylight, he said. He was lost to us, remembering our existence only long enough to inform Sonya that he couldn't possibly afford for both of them to stay overnight in the hotel, and we three had better go right away or we'd miss the last bus.

We already had missed it, Misha found out from the woman at the hotel desk, but there was a train half a mile away. Leaving Boris gazing at his waterfall, we dog-trotted and slid on the icy road to the station, and got there just in time to see the train leaving. Two well-dressed men who looked rather like business executives except that they couldn't be, came panting up behind us, and the five of us stood looking sorrowfully at the last puff of smoke.

'Oh, wonderful,' one of the men said at last.

'Marvellous.'

'Oh, my.'

'Mmm.'

'So what now?'

'The hotel I suppose.'

'O-h-h.' A long groan. 'My wife. That's all.'

'*Your* wife!'

'*Bawzhemoi.*'

Together they set out, and we followed behind them back

to the hotel. Just what their conjugal problems were remained obscure.

Boris was sitting on the ground by the waterfall, sketching something in the snow with a stick. 'Oh, you're back,' he said without enthusiasm. He poked some dots into his abstract snow design, looking like a child with his head cocked on one side and the tip of his tongue sticking out.

'There are,' he announced presently, 'no rooms.'

Moaning, the rest of our happy crew collapsed in the snow. 'What a simply great day,' I directed at poor Misha. Then I decided it would be best from everyone's point of view if I could recapture my train-station-stupor, which wasn't hard. Sonya was as helpless as her husband, who himself probably would have sat drawing in the snow all night if we hadn't come back. Sensing the complete lack of co-operation and community spirit in his team, Misha, martyred, staggered back into the hotel, and reappeared several minutes later with a business-like air.

'Those men have rooms, of course. What do you do to people, you imbecile?' he added to Boris, who shrugged and drew on. 'That woman is in such a state! Well, there are no rooms anyway. The men must have bribed her or something, but I have exactly fifty roubles.' Not enough for rooms, much less anything else. 'So.'

Eventually, after everything had sunk in and he got no response from anyone, he went on, 'Well, I *have* done something anyway. A lot of thanks I get. The woman has a friend who will put us up. Over there,' he pointed. He pulled Boris up, Sonya and I followed, and we crossed the road. There was a big archway and some cottages on the other side. Spread across the arch was a sign.

'Wow!' said Boris, or the Russian equivalent. 'The Ministry of Defence! Ha! ha-ha. Our *Amerikanka* is going to spend the night in the Ministry of Defense holiday resort! "No admittance except authorized personnel." Wow!'

This almost made the day worth it.

We followed Misha to a little bungalow near the entrance.

In answer to his knock, a man came to the door and said that the woman we wanted wasn't home yet—she had gone to the movies. So we sat down and waited. Some thirty minutes later the woman returned, Misha explained the situation to her, and she seemed pleased that we should stay to bring in some extra money. She opened the door and a weird hysterical whistling noise approached us—it was some sort of noise-maker being blown by a boy with a face like a monster. He blew shriekingly back into the other room when he saw us, and re-emerged a moment later with three other smaller children, all with the same monster face.

We were shown into a small cosy kitchen, where a man (introduced as the woman's brother) and his wife sat around a table drinking tea. The house had looked deceptively big from the outside. In fact it was a small two-roomed cabin, which the woman's husband had built himself. He had been a carpenter but was dead now, she told us. She showed us a blurred photograph of a Slavic face.

I was Misha's cousin, just arrived from Tallinn, and Estonian was the strange language we spoke together, it was explained. The woman had never heard English apparently, and in fact had never encountered a language barrier before. She was fascinated to meet someone she couldn't speak to.

We went into the bedroom which would be ours for the night, while the family would sleep on cots in the kitchen. It hadn't seemed nearly big enough for them all, but it was too late to start asking questions. The bedroom had a rustic look; it was full of crude home-made chairs and chests, plus two small beds and a big bedstead with lace covers. In the centre was a whitewashed furnace with its chimney disappearing through the ceiling. Her husband had done everything, the woman said, even the pictures. There were three quite good primitives on the walls, one of Boris's waterfall. He had already discovered them, and was leaping about with his old ecstasy again.

'Isn't it *wonderful*, Sonya! Wonderful, wonderful, wonderful. Not a single portrait of Lenin as a child, and these are quite wonderful. I should like to stay here,' he broached. 'I should like to buy this and stay here. Sonya?' Long-suffering Sonya looked at him patiently and tried to distract him with something else.

The four monster children stood around and gawped at us, sucking their thumbs and taking turns persecuting a very fat dog they had. The mother came and took them away after they got in a fight over the dog. We four were given basins of water to wash in and shown where the outside privy was; then we went to sleep in beautiful feather beds.

At seven the next morning, the eldest monster blew reveille on its noise-maker. Boris leaped out of bed and would have strangled him but for the joint intervention of the mother and Sonya. We had to get up then. The others had already gone to work, and the woman said she would be glad to make us breakfast. She had already baked some bread and would get us fresh milk from her neighbour's cow if we would watch the children. Boris wasn't interested; he left to find some paper for his waterfall sketch. Misha went out with two pails to bring some fresh water, and Sonya amused the children in the kitchen.

The eldest found me alone in the bedroom making beds. He crept stealthily up behind me, blew his nasty whistle, and when I had catapulted around in terror, said in perfect English: 'I do not understand why you say you are Estonian.' With a hideous leer which came out vocally in some sort of very original noise, he skipped out of the room.

I wished Boris hadn't been restrained that morning. There was no way of keeping it from Misha; the little boy, having succeeded with his exercise in surprise timing, spilled all the beans to everyone over breakfast. Though he tried his best to hide it, Misha was scared. The Ministry of Defence! He talked to me later, after Sonya had gone off to find Boris.

We walked through the village, past neat cottages with columns of smoke drifting perpendicularly up from their tops, then down to the water to look at Finland again. He argued with himself: 'Will anything happen? No, of course not! But that boy, how stupid! He learns English in school, of course. Ministry of Defence. *Nu?* But if he tells . . . But how could it matter? Why am I so selfish? I am afraid of you, of what will happen to me because of you. Me, me, me. Isn't it all so stupid?' He laughed. 'Of course they know anyway if they want to know. And the others, besides. Did you see that man in the blue coat and grey cap in the café before we left last night? I think he may have overheard us and followed us to the bus. I wasn't sure it was the same one, it was dark, maybe not. I wanted to ask you but he was gone then and I didn't want you to worry. Yes, anyway, they know.'

'But what can happen? Everyone tells me—you too—that this is over.'

'Yes, I know. That is what I mean about being selfish. It is very important for all of us to build things as they should be. But I am selfishly afraid—there is so much to lose, for my parents and me. And sometimes these things do not go well. Yesterday . . .' He stopped.

'What yesterday?'

'Well, yesterday . . . I telephoned to one of my friends—he has many contacts in the organization. I wanted to know how it was. He said that it could be bad for me, very bad, but that nothing would happen until you went away. That is the way they work—so you wouldn't hear of it. He said that they must know, because all such things they know. I have been trying to think of something I could tell them. I think . . . that we met in the Hermitage, perhaps, by accident. You asked me a question, and then I . . .'

'But why can't you tell the truth? There isn't anything *wrong*. What's *wrong?*'

'Well, we must not think, we shall forget about it. Yes?'

Ten seconds later he had stopped forgetting. 'What if something does. I must get word to you.' He thought. 'I will telephone every Sunday morning, that's it. And if something happens, Boris will telephone instead. He will say I am sick. You understand?'

This had reached such proportions that it was impossible

to go on. I tried to think of anything to change the subject, but nothing came to my head.

'How wonderful that snow is *white*,' I finally said cheerfully. 'I'm so glad it's white.'

'Sometimes it's blue,' he answered, trying too. 'Sometimes out here, when the sun is shining—oh, it hurts your eyes to look at it, it's so bright and blue and beautiful . . .'

I thought about it and shivered.

'Are you cold?'

'No, I was having a dream. About mountains in Switzerland. I always wanted to go. Rich people in England go every winter—and I was dreaming—that I was rich, and then I'd go to Switzerland, and you would be there too.'

'No, it is impossible.'

'Why? It's a *dream*, I told you. Everything is possible in my dream. Really, I couldn't go any more than you.'

'Of course you can. You can do anything when you're free. Anything. You could go with no money, money isn't important, you could work. I would work, I would be a servant, if that was all. Anywhere! How it must be . . . An ocean, a big ocean, and *heat!* Sun, such sun—and—an island, in the ocean. I can't imagine what they're like. I think of it, my sun shining on this ocean, perhaps a boat . . . Ah, you have no idea! If only I didn't—if only I was a *kolkhoznik* and didn't read or imagine. Ah, why am I saying these things?' Suddenly he was furious. 'Some day it will come true! And perhaps we will meet in Switzerland!' He jumped up, and we ran back up the road.

We caught a train back to the city, after saying goodbye to Boris and Sonya. They had almost no money, Misha had spent all his on our night, and I had only just enough for our fares, so what they would do seemed a little doubtful at that point. But Boris was too preoccupied with his waterfall to worry. I saw him briefly in Moscow a month later, and he said they had got lifts on the backs of a couple of trucks. That was very old history by then though—he was crazy with energy after selling a few pictures at last. The waterfall was one of them; it was a big success.

Misha and I spent the hours before my train's departure at the Hermitage, trying to get into an exhibition of ancient Scythian treasure. They wouldn't let me in without a passport. Then a ride to the Petropavlovsk Fortress, and a walk around the beautiful city, and finally the last meal of the condemned at the Astoria. The depression stayed with us and was aggravated by the restaurant. It was very cold and empty, except for three or four lone men sitting at strategic intervals around the room. They all seemed to be staring at us. And there were other eyes too: spot-lights in each corner of the ceiling, rotating, rotating, even though their lights were turned off because the band wasn't there. With the sense of conspiracy that pervaded everything they seemed human, watching. With one in each corner they couldn't miss a thing.

Back at the station, I was as ready as Misha to examine my suitcase. Of course it was impossible to tell if it had been tampered with because it had got disarranged just in being carried. Misha wouldn't have made a much better spy than I.

He wanted to be very careful about seeing me off: train platforms were invitations to doom. He told a story. A friend of his who had been in Moscow during the festival had fallen in love with a French girl. He had seen her every day and no one had found out, until he had gone to the station to say good-bye to her. He had kissed her on the platform. Later, after she was gone and he was going back home, he realized that he was being followed by a man who had been standing around at the station. If he led the man back to his house he would be identified. So he chased frantically through the metro, boarding trains as the doors shut and leaving them at the last minute, but the man stayed with him. It soon became so obvious, even to the pursuer, that he gave up trying to conceal himself, and the two of them ran all over Moscow silently challenging each other. After hours of it, Misha's friend almost decided to call it quits and try to speak to the man, talk him out of it, but he realized that in keeping up the chase he had incriminated himself. Then his opportunity came to get free, and other questions had to be left hanging. He got on a moving tram at a run and as the pursuer barely made it on at another door, he dropped off again and ducked behind a fence, down an alley and through miles of the maze of old Moscow streets.

'But they probably took his photograph at the station anyway, so it didn't really matter,' Misha ended mournfully.

Whenever I heard stories of this kind, as I did frequently, there was always the question at the end that I asked but never got more than a shrug for an answer. So what would have happened if they *had* caught him?

Misha kissed me goodbye too, but not on the platform. We walked quietly to the train, I got on, and we stood there looking at each other stupidly while uproarious farewells took place all around us.

Misha, alone and tragic. Everything was so horrible! I was still very much a Marsman, who had entered another world and created nothing but havoc and destruction. Something awful would happen to Misha, I would never see him again, but at that stage I was hardly frightened by the idea. I had lived with it long enough to become absolutely sure of it. I was wrong.

Nichevo

As THE MIDNIGHT TRAIN slipped away I heard someone behind me say, 'Yes wait, we'll get some sandwiches.' Sandwiches, sandwiches, sandwiches . . . For the second time, overhearing English, it took a moment for it to come into focus. The echoed word repeated itself in my head, then suddenly filled me with fabulous joy—sandwiches: English: two people, at least, who weren't mice and weren't afraid of cats.

The voices belonged to an Indian and a Canadian. I fell on them, almost literally, and after they had recovered and learned my nationality, they explained that they were part of a delegation of nuclear physicists on their way back to Moscow after a tourist trip to Leningrad. They had been invited for a conference and were due to go home soon. Leading me back to the buffet, they mentioned that there were two Americans with them, as well as English, French, Germans, Africans, and practically everything.

Meeting the Americans, I felt a mixture of apprehension and old-home-week corn. 'Hi! Where're you from?'—as only Americans away from America do it, on a Moscow-bound train—would inevitably lead to that moment of tension when the implicit questions started to form in everyone's minds. After the last few days, I was filled with the conviction that absolutely everybody was out to get somebody else, and now it would be them, and me, because of the China thing. But it never came to that. After a brief show of curiosity, their warmth and humour, the American, French, Indian, and every other brand, had me and kept me submerged half that night. We drank beer and ate tangerines, discussed our homes, people, the latest jokes and the latest shows, books, events, and not until the table was smothered in peel and I felt real again did we go to bed.

In my compartment were a very prosperous-looking Russian couple and a Polish student. This was the Red Arrow, a classy train—more expensive, faster, with a bar, mattresses that fit, a functioning washroom, and no music. All the people on it were classy too. The Pole and I sympathized with each other over our allotment of compartment-mates, who simply sat quite still and glared at us. They were dressed in furs, fat and stuffy in a Western bourgeois way, and prudish in a special Russian way. Their prudery made them leave the carriage when I lit a cigarette. It was not that smoking bothered them —the husband did it—but females smoking definitely did. What really infuriated them though were my blue jeans. I hardly dared wear them in the Moscow streets because of the leers they earned from passers-by. On one particularly memorable excursion I had taken in slacks, a woman screamed 'Prostitute!' (why?) and another spat at me. (A sleeveless dress had had nearly the same inexplicable effect on Chinese peasants the summer before.) Anyway, now I wore my jeans, mainly because of the cold but partly out of sheer nastiness, to annoy the Russian couple. Early the next morning, soon after they had viewed the disgusting sight of me, they packed up their bags and made off down the train corridor. The Polish student approved of this manœuvre; he congratulated me and gave an excellent imitation of the couple's waddling scorn. After a few minutes of gradually subsiding hysterics, we began to talk about politics and world conditions. Does it always infallibly work out that Westerners talk about little things and Easterners about big things—even their jokes? Maybe, anyway it occurred to me then.

The Pole had nothing but the most withering contempt for

all things Russian. I had heard that all Poles did, that they traditionally divided their hatred between the Germans and the Russians, but somehow didn't expect it then. I thought that one representing his country in the Soviet Union would at least be unaggressive about his loathing, if not downright safe. The Hungarians, for instance, had sent to the festival only the most loyal of their youth, only those who supported the fascist-uprising version of their revolution.

This man told me at length how much things had improved in Poland 'since October'. He used the phrase with the same frequency as the Chinese 'before liberation' and 'since liberation'. His political philosophy rested almost entirely on doubt; on the one hand he felt that Poland could never thrive under any régime but a socialist one, on the other that the changes for the better since October had mainly been in the opposite direction. His primary concern was freedom, though, and he assured me that few other ideas preoccupied the Poles he knew. They wanted freedom, and they didn't want anything with the slightest Russian tinge to it. 'The Russians? Quite simply—barbarians!' he shrugged, almost with pity. 'But we need them, that is the trouble. The Germans . . .' He laughed. 'The Russians kill half my family, the Germans kill the other half, but anyway I prefer a Mercedes to a Zim.'

Remembering the other Poles I had met, particularly a young boy in Poznan when we had made a half-hour stop there on the original London-Moscow festival trip, I thought that their very resistance and impetuosity, so unlike the Russian attitude, won part of their freedom struggle for them. The boy in Poznan had taken me for a twenty-five minute running tour around his city, and had plunged right in immediately to describe his very active part in the Poznan uprising. He spoke as he pleased, as did all the others, and wasn't affected in the least with fear or even caution with strangers. Life's too short, and they insisted on screaming loudly at any grievance, bashing their way forward regardless of consequences. When that happens in numbers, consequences must be fewer anyway.

Moscow again. Home again. It looked uglier than it ever had, and very monotonously grey and cold. Those skyscrapers. Those madly unintentional brick patterns, where the builders had run out of one colour and had started another. Oh dear, what about Misha? The taxi driver was telling me some story about his experiences at the front in the war. He appeared to recognize me. I couldn't concentrate—a new crisis had occurred to me, financial this time: my rent was due, Dunya had to be paid, and there were other bills. You couldn't pay anything by cheque. Cash it had to be, and delivered. No amount of calculating or recounting seemed to indicate that there was even enough to pay the taxi. The driver drew up outside my apartment house and I gave him the good news. Fourteen roubles on the meter—I had eight. But he didn't care at all. He grinned and said, 'Oh *that's* all right,' just as if it happened every day, 'You give it to me when you have it, I see you around a lot, it's a pleasure!' He wouldn't even tell me his name, and drove off before I could look back inside at the sign giving it.

I called up my office to see if I could get paid some of the money they owed me. This wasn't always easy; like all offices they had only certain times when cash was available (in their case twice a month) and even then it meant queuing three times, filling out forms, getting the right signatures, and, for lack of a passport, a witness to vouch for my identity. They said they'd try and I should come down. Any vague hitch in anything required the hour's journey there to straighten out—nothing could be arranged over the phone with them or anybody else. This time there was certainly no alternative, though it might be in vain. But I hadn't even a few kopecks for the fare, and there wasn't anyone at home to borrow from. Then I remembered hearing about the disgraceful problem of the hooligans who pretend to have passes and don't pay their bus fares, and decided to become a temporary hooligan. I put on my best Russian outfit, heavy brown stockings, thick scarf, mittens, and a dark coat I had used before mine arrived, and set out.

The first one was easy. It was so crowded that I could squeeze unobserved to the rear corner. Nothing makes me more nervous than trying to cheat someone out of a few kopecks, or pence, or cents. If it were a really colossal crime it wouldn't be so bad. I imagined my guilt was absolutely obvious, and that everybody was looking at me and whispering to their friends about the hooliganka. How quickly one can absorb the most full-grown persecution complex! No one bothered me though. Then I had to take a tram—the metro was out, with its foolproof ticket system. The tram unfortunately wasn't crowded, but while the conductor was coping with something else I snuck in behind her. Three stops later she started yelling at me. I could never understand Russian when it was unpleasant. Anyway, I did understand and didn't understand, but she wasn't having any either way. She came over to my seat and started joggling me, then really letting me have it with every inch of vocal cord she possessed. I looked at her as angelically as I could—and she made me get out.

The frost layer was a couple of inches deep on the windows that day, and it wasn't the ideal weather for a stroll. The coat I had used for my disguise of inconspicuousness had no lining. Still, after trying to ride three more times with results all approximately the same, there was no choice but to walk it. There was only a mile or so left anyway. But it was so cold. Few people were out, and those who were walked hurriedly with their faces down and swathed in scarves. The squares seemed twice as long as they ever had before, and even before they had seemed twice as long as squares anywhere else. I invented a song to help with the time and the cold.

SNOW
MOSCOW
Ho Ho

Just as I was passing the Lenin Library, I heard a whistling and screeching commotion behind me. Another accident near-miss. But I turned and a taxi pulled up to the kerb. It was my friend from the morning!

'You see?' he said, 'it didn't take long, did it?'

I told him I was going to get his money, stretching it rather, and he insisted on taking me there. This time I got his name, just in case I didn't bump into him again. But I did, a week later, and again after that quite a few times. He was always so pleased to have a foreigner to talk to that it was a job making him accept money at all.

The Foreign Languages Publishing House was an interesting place. It wasn't just a business, but a very large organization taking care of most compartments of its employees' lives. Since a large proportion of the employees were foreigners who could never in millions of years fathom the intricacies and vagaries of Russian red tape—and who cared where Russians didn't—they needed quite a lot done for them. A special member of the staff spent his time going mad over the various problems that foreigners in Moscow were prone to, including lodging, shopping, postal, language, financial and legal difficulties. The publishing house, through him, took care of me down to the last pillow case, which he delivered all the way to my flat personally in his chauffeur-driven car.

Outside the office then hung a big red-and-white *Agitpunkt* banner, as on many buildings all over the city. There was to be a minor election soon, and this was one of the agitation centres. Quite a few of my friends were agitators, even Shura, who found it handy to shield some of his more frowned-on activities. Every evening he went around to various houses assigned to him where he gave pep-talks to the good citizens on how splendid their government was and why they should vote *da*. I asked him to take me with him once, but though he viewed the whole thing with the utmost cynicism he couldn't go that far.

In the courtyard, a few stenographers and sub-editors were skating on a bumpy improvised ring. Inside, past a knitting receptionist and a cloakroom, was a long corridor where groups of people stood about and gossiped in every conceivable language. The house published books for almost every foreign country, and these people, the translators and editors, were from everywhere. The hall was like a permanent international cocktail party, except that there weren't any drinks. The long wall behind them was covered with multi-lingual wall newspapers, slogans, graphs showing progress or non-progress of the last Plan, articles about how to improve the style of work, notices of meetings and activities. Today there was to be an important meeting, I gathered from scraps of talk I overheard.

I wove my way through the conversations to the English Department and collected a few promises relating to my pay. Wait, that was all. I found a group of Englishmen to wait with; they were always very friendly and eager to talk to a new foreign figure. They were so few that they were figures. Like the colony in Peking, the foreigners living in Moscow stuck together quite a lot, but though they were very interesting I was there specifically to meet Russians, so I didn't get to know them very well. A lot of them had lived there for decades and were citizens, but were still essentially foreign in outlook and humour.

This group, like the others, was discussing the meeting, and everyone was in such an advanced stage of feeling that it took a while to unearth what it was all about. A young Russian, who had been an editor and was promoted to translator, had earned 7,000 roubles for a new translation of Gogol's *Dead Souls*. On the basis of this windfall he had got married, bought new clothes, and was living very prosperously. All had gone well with him until a control editor, checking his work, realized that the English was far too colloquial for him to have done, and from there soon discovered that he had copied an old translation almost word for word. Everyone was yelling about what a foul trick this was, and give-him-hell. Someone pointed him out to me. He was standing like an outcast at the end of the hall, looking absolutely forlorn and wretched in his new fur coat.

The meeting was about to begin. Everyone was involved,

including the people I was waiting for, so I went downstairs to the assembly room too. The culprit sat alone on one side; the witnesses left him surrounded by empty chairs as if he had an infectious disease. Behind a table the department head started reading a report of the incident in a droning monotone. The man slumped forward in his seat, twisting a hat-check ticket and pulling at his hair, as each transgression was intoned and the general outcry grew. The audience became more and more emotional. Some, who had been shouting loudest before, looked almost compassionate. Father mercilessly beating son, but this hurts me more than it hurts you. Others were less complicatedly furious. Eventually the verdict: he was fired and had a couple of weeks to return all the money. This was fair, except that he'd spent the money, and losing his job so discreditably meant it would be entered in his record and he wouldn't be able to get another one. But he wasn't called on to give his side.

Filing upstairs again, the group was still tense and arguing. I said that the only thing I could blame him for was his stupidity in not doing the thing well if he had to do it. Shocked stares. They were right, of course. Then I suggested that if he were reinstated he certainly would never do it again, that this would permanently ruin his life. A few agreed, but it didn't matter now. The man shuffled out of the building, almost physically propelled by the condemnation darting from the scores of pairs of eyes aimed at him.

My money came through with revolutionary speed, and after another half hour no more crisis. A friend who had been at the meeting, an international character, mainly Egyptian, volunteered to buy me dinner. He had lived in the Soviet Union for some time as an Arabic translator, but at some stage in his career had picked up terribly American English. We went to the Peking Hotel and ate imitation Chinese food with chopsticks (he had lived in China too), forgot about the meeting, and talked about *small* things. The restaurant wouldn't be full till later on, and in the meantime there were only a few people there, all solemnly attending to the business of eating—while our table roared and rocked, an oasis of gaiety. Although it was a Chinese meal conducted in a foreign spirit, it lasted a Russian mealtime; three hours later we staggered out full of enough food to last weeks.

While we were in the neighbourhood, the Egyptian said he had some small business to transact. We went into a furniture store full of nothing but pianos and he discussed something in the back with the saleswoman.

'I've been trying to get a new armchair,' he explained as we left. 'It's hard to tell when they might come in again, so I've been cultivating this gal to save me one when they do. Costs a hundred roubles extra but it's worth it—had to get all my furniture that way but my place looks fine now. This city is really okay when you learn the system. You just gotta learn the system, is all.'

The system you gotta learn, he went on, includes not being browbeaten by the petty race of people around. Go to the TOP! See the guy in CHARGE! Or threaten to sign the book. There is a complaints book in all hotels, stores, or any place where you pay for service. The system gets slightly more complicated when it's a case of not-paying—no book, and a good deal of energy needed before you can get to that guy in charge. But where there's a book there's a way. It is for comments, good or bad, though it is rarely actually written in—the threat is what counts. Apparently everyone has a horror of some adverse criticism going down in writing, there for the world and the manager to see, so just the tiniest, politest hint that you would please like the book causes major character reformations.

We passed a record store and I remembered that I wanted some particular ones so we went in. Like a bookshop it was full of people, and the most incredible noise. There were no sound-proof booths, only not-very-local loudspeakers distributed at intervals, and about fifteen different sorts of music blended into a hideous cacophony. Swarms of people surrounded each counter, pushing and shoving to get their hands on the record index, and around the popular dance music section a regular stampede was going on. The crowd around us became even more so when they saw the dark-skinned Egyptian—everybody wanted to see him and touch him. 'They see so few non-whites that some of them have the idea that the colour rubs off!' laughed my friend. 'They're curious, but they like us. The woman who cleans my place—the first day when she was making the bed—looked all over it and in it to see if I'd turned the sheets brown.' We got royal service. Records are about the most economical items on sale, only five or ten roubles for a long-player, so we each bought dozens.

Outside we parted, and I headed homewards to get some sleep. The snow had been falling for some time, and the streets were blustery white. The time of the year, the foreignness of the day, and the sound of an accordion in the distance, made me think of Christmas and carols, and I sang some to myself on the way home. I even tried infecting the sour-faced woman at the bottom of the elevator with my Christmas spirit, and she practically smiled. What could be better in the nice nice world than everything was? I thought, riding upstairs and reaching for my key. It wasn't there. My purse wasn't there, with my money in it, and the key. Not all the money though— rouble notes are so enormous that, in quantity, they don't fit into just one wallet and have to be distributed. That was something, anyway. Pick-pocketed—in that crowded record store. A hooligan . . . ? Served me right.

I rang the bell. There wouldn't be any trouble, it was just as if the lock had been changed again, and there were rarely less than ten Greeks hanging around waiting to find their gaps on the floor. But after a few minutes, when no one answered, I realized that there wasn't even one single Greek. I went next door to Dunya's. Three sets of people lived there, and the usual notice hung by the door: ring once for X, twice for Y, three times for Z. Dunya was twice, but no answer. I tried once. A woman came to the door saying that Dunya had gone to church, keys and all. I sat on my coat on the stairs waiting for someone to turn up, and tried to edit some of a manuscript I had with me, but there wasn't enough light. So I sang some more carols, until the end of my repertoire. I was afraid I would start worrying about Misha, so to fill up more time I worked out a routine about Snow Moscow Ho Ho, Moscow ho snow oh ho ho, ho snow Moscow no snow ho, oh ho no ho snow Moscow, oh ho oh ho oh ho HO.

Fifteen minutes, thirty minutes, fifty. The elevator creaked into motion, but it stopped below on the ninth floor. There weren't many variations left on the ho ho song. Then Dunya's door opened and the same woman came out again. She couldn't imagine what was keeping Dunya, and showed her concern for my plight by ringing my doorbell a few times. She shook her head sympathetically, then went back in. A while later she reappeared and suggested that I wait inside where I'd be more comfortable. She successfully battled what little resistance I could work up, and I followed her in. It was completely dark. Only then I realized that she was blind. She had just one of the rooms in the flat, she said, and some of her neighbours would be glad to have me watch television with them. She knocked on their door and after they had heard about it they opened it wide to me, pleased and smiling to have someone to entertain. No people come close to beating the Russians at hospitality. No other people give so much of what they have with so little self-consciousness about how poor it might be.

The room was typical—most of it was bed. There was a big double one, a single, and a cot surrounding that round table with that fringed lamp hovering over it. A wardrobe and cabinet for dishes and food were somehow squeezed into the remaining space, and a TV set (small screen with a huge round magnifying glass attached to the front) sat importantly in the corner. Everything was covered with lace. In this lived a young couple with their small boy and girl, and *babushka,* who took care of the housework and children while her daughter worked. In this family situation, like so many others, the whole structure rested on the grandmother, and without her, order, and practically their very existence, would have collapsed. If the younger woman had had to stay at home and be housewife and mother, there would have been only half the income and even more of a space problem than there already was. Motherhood has to skip a generation.

There was a very funny comedian named Rykin on the television, then a film which went too fast for me, then a few other things. The family was as addicted as their counterparts elsewhere, and kept the room in semi-darkness and complete silence while they clustered round the set. 'Sh' the boy said to the girl when she laughed too long. 'Ssshh!' Only the grandmother, who wasn't interested, pottered about, then went out to the communal kitchen to prepare tea. At 10.30 came the final theme music, and it was the end of television for the day. Still no Dunya, still no Greeks. The family insisted that I stay; the women were really upset about the awful catastrophe that they felt overwhelmed me, and did their best to ease my sufferings. As poor as they were, they were determined to feed me, and offered 'tea' in a tone that didn't admit the possibility of refusal. As usual, I didn't want feeding, the Chinese dinner had fixed that, and I used some advice I had been given that Russians consider one refusal politeness, two refusals real politeness, but three you mean it. I tried three and more, but my protestations got me nowhere. They brought out everything they had for me, but ate almost nothing themselves. It was a new adventure: their first foreigner. The children sat on the floor staring hard at me, as if I would melt into a dream if they stopped. And their parents asked me about America and England—was it as cold as this there, and what did people eat, was it true how high the rents were, was the English queen pretty, were they dishonest in America (after I told them that I thought I'd been pickpocketed), and what did you do for holidays? On their holiday that summer they had all been at a Black Sea resort run by the husband's factory; it was almost free and they had been able to go swimming in the sea! Then followed photographs of the holiday, photographs of the children, their relatives from Rostov, and anything else they could find to show me. And how much did you pay for your shoes? the woman asked. I told her and asked what hers had cost. Three hundred roubles, she said (which is about triple the price of English or American shoes).

'Don't you think that's rather high?' I said, wondering what she felt about prices.

'We understand that it is high, of course, but the little too much that we pay we know is for the welfare of the country.'

I asked her what she wanted most, and she said, 'More or less what I already have—a good job, leisure now and then, the opportunity to study—and peace, peace in the world is what I want for me and my children.' She thought a bit. 'I would like a new flat . . .'

And all the time, while the young mother and father plied me with questions and the children looked and looked, *babushka* brought more food. It got later and their anxiety increased. At last they offered me one of their beds, and that was an order, like the food. Just as the situation was getting out of hand, I heard the elevator stop and sounds of Greek laughter resounding through the hall. At the same time, Dunya appeared—she had gone to someone's house after church.

I thanked my new friends. They really were friends, too, like the taxi driver earlier—to a degree that would have taken years of careful building anywhere else.

Just at midnight, as I went to bed, the Greeks started singing and dancing. *Nichevo*, ho ho. That's what twenty-four hours in Russia could be like.

★

12

The Memory of the Heart

TIME WENT BY. I worked hard to get ahead of myself, then slid, and spent days with people, days of doing and discussing. Time made all sense of strangeness disappear. I began to absorb Russian values, understand more about the people, and stop noticing differences. Everything fitted, and so did I, and life was much the same for me as for permanent Muscovites, or for anybody anywhere adjusted into habit patterns.

Sometimes there was newness. Just being foreign, in a country that had a shortage of foreigners, paid many dividends. I was asked to play an English girl in a Russian film. That state of Anglo-Saxonness did it; no one seemed to mind that it was my sole qualification. I couldn't act, but then this was the land where 'ever-r-rybody can do ever-r-rything', as my festival interpreter had said, that non-believer in brains or talent.

The Memory of the Heart was its name. It was the story of an English pilot who crashed in the Soviet Union during the war, whose life was saved by a woman and a boy—two partisans near the enemy lines. Long afterwards in England he remembered the Russians with affection, told his friends about his experiences, and resolved to go back and find the two his heart remembered. The big English scene was our hero's birthday party at his home in the London suburbs, with eleven members of his family celebrating and hearing about Russian courage. The idea, of building a non-political bridge between Western and Eastern peoples, raised a big cheer from me.

142

Throughout, they were using a new language technique: the Germans in the battle scenes, and the English later, spoke German and English instead of accented Russian, with a Russian translation dubbed in louder than the voices. In principle it seemed a fine plan, but they couldn't unearth enough English people in our case to prevent the final group from sounding and looking rather lopsided. Seven had to be played by Russians, two of whom spoke no English whatsoever and the others in varying stages of shakiness, but in any case the members of our 'family' were a diverse enough lot to have modelled for practically all the facial types.

It was all a marvellous try, but there were problems. The Russian conception of an English home, and costumes, and birthday party, and English dialogue at a birthday party, was —Russian. The right props for the set were mostly unavailable, so what there was had to be shifted around to be background whatever the camera angle. The place was littered with dummy G-plan, Penguins, old *Good Housekeepings* and *Looks*, a real dog, a stuffed toy lion, reproductions of abstract art, a model of a sailing ship, any other rather alien-looking objects that turned up, and a golden Limoges coffee set, insured for 30,000 roubles, reposing grandly among the makeshift. The costumes were made by the studio seamstress who didn't do at all badly considering the odds; she had access to foreign fashion magazines and Russian fabrics, quite beautiful, which I had never seen on sale. For shoes we went to Gum, where I discovered there was a special section way up on top that made things to order for those unlikely few who might be able to afford it. There, they had two models of ultra-fashionable shoes (for 600 roubles a pair) and a few impossibly expensive samples of cloth. A special shoemaker meticulously measured my feet for the only custom-made shoes I was ever likely to get, and produced them two days late and two sizes too small.

The whole thing was completely *mad*, but I think most of that was movies and not Soviet movies. Certainly there were many very Soviet aspects to it though, such as the fact that since it happened to be the beginning of the month when we started shooting our scene, no one did anything. Everyone knew that a certain amount of work had to be completed to fulfil the Plan, but since scores weren't added up until the end of the month everyone took it easy; then during the last few days work went on till 3 or 4 a m in frenzied scramble. But there we were at the month's beginning, there I was with my great career as a movie star about to begin, and no one did anything at all, and no one even remotely cared. After reaching the studio, tearing into our costumes and being smeared with make-up on every bare surface (which was a lot of square footage, as the Russians, who don't expose much skin, believed the English went in for a good deal of décolletage), and proudly considering ourselves ready for the big moment, we spent seven hours waiting. We couldn't move much without wrecking the make-up. The others, including three Englishmen, were so conditioned to this sort of thing that they didn't consider it necessary to ask what the insurmountable difficulty might be, but there wasn't really anyone to ask anyway because no one knew. So we sat and talked, or when conversation flagged, explored the place (slowly, because of the make-up).

There was nothing particularly grand about the studio, to someone used to associating grandness with the movie world, and no one with inflated Hollywood-type ideas. It was just another organization like the publishing house. A militiaman at the door let those people in who had passes. There were miles of corridors weaving in and out, with conference rooms and costume, prop, and make-up rooms leading off, all very bare. The canteen, which often cleverly managed to shut itself at mealtimes, contained a few rather old caviar sandwiches, now and then some borshch or sausages or *kefir*, a bunch of grubby tables, a grubby cafeteria counter, and a grubby woman presiding. The people in it, or wandering around the halls, were mainly White Guards that month for some other film, all with orange faces.

Eventually we progressed as far as our sound stage, where

we still sat, but with a change of scenery. It was a few hundred snow-covered yards from the rest of the studio, a big barn of a place and fabulously cold. The woman in charge of the sound-recording room kept us amused by playing Ella Fitzgerald records. My worst moment was when somebody discovered that I knew the words to *Rock Around the Clock*, because from then on I had to sing it to everybody there. 'Everybody' looked like about a hundred people. They were all sitting too, except for brief spurts of activity over something on the set. All its contents were held together and propped up quite ingeniously with wire, bits of bricks, and hope. The camera had a metal plaque on its side reading 'Made in Hollywood, usa'. It was my friend—made the same place as me and looking about as old.

In fact everyone was everyone's friend, I saw when we got started. It was another one of those times when international co-operation looks easy. Each person tried genuinely to ease the others' lot, and after I got used to the utterly casual approach to the whole movie I realized that there were a lot more important things anyway. Kindness and good spirits were never in a more concentrated form. I think the theme of the film, the emphasis on common international bonds, was perhaps the most basic thing behind the seeking of common individual bonds as well.

Anyway, finally at midnight of the second day, the filming began. We assembled around the dinner table, rehearsed a few lines twenty-odd times, then shot them six times. The next day the wall was taken down and moved round to the back together with the Penguins and stuffed lion, the camera and all the lights were shifted, and exactly the same thing repeated from a different angle—after another twenty rehearsals. Finally they tore the table in half to get close-ups. After repeating the same spontaneous laugh fifty times nothing seemed at all laughable, even the Englishman next to me describing the disgusting drink they had given us for port as 'distilled animosity'. We had to drink it anyway, and we had to eat cake. If the Russians hadn't much of a clear idea about the English, the one thing they did know was that the English always had cakes at their birthday parties. To lend that last word in authenticity, it was essential to have a cake on the table all the time with candles flaring. It was a huge, very Russian cake, with 'Many Happy Returns' scrawled across the top, and it had to be eaten at each rehearsal and each take. The eating was one thing, but the candles were a real undertaking. They were huge ones, which hissed down to nothing in no time. To keep them constantly burning, literally scores of people were kept in a state of pandemonium, pulling burnt ones out and shoving new ones in, holding their breath in case they went out before the scene was shot, and worrying that the roaring noise they made in the silence might spoil the soundtrack. 'A new simile,' one Russian said in delight: 'Roaring like a candle!'

Under the table, and everywhere out of the camera's vision, was chaos. Above the set on a hanging shelf two men, oblivious of the uproar below, slept or played dominoes in fifteen-minute intervals when they weren't occupied with klieg lights. People people people, everywhere milling around, powdering noses and combing wigs, measuring, shoving bits of wood under shaky table legs, sawing off chunks of scenery that interfered with the camera, moving camera tracks, endlessly running back and forth with cake, and all frantically, expertly, getting in each other's way as much as anyone could. Then suddenly, the régisseur announced the Russian equivalent of 'Lights . . . camera . . . *action!*' and silence, not a breath, while my friend the camera did its stuff. Over and over and over and over.

On top of everything, the lights kept exploding. One, dangling precariously over our heads like a sword of Damocles, thundered pieces of glass all over the set. Glass in the coffee, in the cake, in the distilled animosity. For days we were all finding splinters in our hair and embedded in our underwear. But the Limoges coffee set, the chief care, was untouched, so there was little anxiety. The blood on the table was all right, they said—it looked like spilt coffee, and since it was a black-and-white film anyway no one would notice the colour.

The way the lines eventually came out was marvellous. The English grandmother didn't know a word of English, and was rather too old to learn such a new trick. Her only line was 'Don't pay too much attention to those plans of Ralph's, George, I've been hearing about this trip for years.' No one will ever forget that line. The whole cast took turns coaching her for hours and hours of days and days, but it just wasn't any good. The final delivery is unwriteable, but it was something like 'Dawnt peh too moch attyenshon to dos plens of R-R-R-Ralph'th Geor-r-rdge, Ay've beeeen hear-r-reeng aibout dees tr-r-reep for year-r-rth,' none of it with any particular intonation but lasting about five minutes before the poor thing, with an expression of immense concentration and suffering on her face, could get it out.

The only other person who knew no English at all had less trouble; she had a shorter line and youth on her side. She was a beautiful woman who knew how to make the best of herself; it turned out she had lived abroad. Despite looks and charm, she kept almost entirely to herself from the beginning, and no one else tried very hard. Once she was standing with a group of us and one man attempted an analysis—she knew she was being discussed but, not understanding, assumed it was complimentary, and smiled and blushed while he talked. 'I've seen hundreds like her,' he said, 'and I'll bet her husband is sick to death of her by now. She's nothing but brittle beauty, and that doesn't mean much here. It's one of the growing pains of socialism, her story—not that I've heard it but I feel I know it all the same. Her husband is probably twenty years older than she is. He was probably a peasant or worker who rose from nothing to be a big rich bureaucrat with something in his head and something in his pocket. His first wife was part of the reason he got there—she slaved for him for twenty-five years, washing his filthy socks and raising his children on no money. But when he gets big, his wife is still Masha the peasant, with no education and having worked too hard to grow intellectually with him. So he throws her over and marries something decorative. Of course this girl—there's a real shortage of men in the Soviet Union—in her age group women outnumber men by more than six to one, and she had to take what there was, but it isn't that. She's a real relic of the past in many ways. All she has ever wanted was money, and she set about seeing that she got it. So she has—but she's bitter now, because it simply doesn't mean what she thought it would.' You can't win.

Christmas drew near, and we occupied the days, before midnight when things got started, trying to teach everyone carols. That evoked little interest. What they really wanted was *Rock Around the Clock* again. 'Sing it! Sing it! *Please* sing it!' I kept on doggedly trying to divert the enthusiasm to carols, but no audience. Christmas nostalgia set in among the English, and we were all rather disappointed when we were told we wouldn't get the day off (it was near the end of the month, of course, and Christmas isn't a holiday in Russia anyway). But we sang between takes, and tried to cheer ourselves up on Christmas Eve when we had to keep on working and it was already three in the morning. At last we filed out forlornly to the dressing room, complaining and unpleasant. But the room was completely transformed from the one we had left hours before: candlelight illuminated a table groaning under the weight of champagne and a party meal preserved from the filmed dinner (cake), there were little presents for everyone, and in the middle a tiny Christmas tree beautifully decorated with film and cotton and scraps of colour. The Russians in the cast and technical crew had improvised it all for our Christmas.

We had a wonderful party, with long emotional toasts and more carols and rocks around clocks. It cemented us all together for good, and as one Englishman with whom I'd been arguing about dreams and realities put it: 'This, you see, is socialism—and Christianity—down to their core. They can be hot air—but they can also be real.'

13

Happy New Year

CHRISTMAS WASN'T A HOLIDAY but the New Year was. Those with religion celebrated the birth of Christ at the end of the first week of January (old-style Julian calendar) but everything else was concentrated on New Year's Eve—gaiety, parties, exchanges of gifts and greeting cards. The shopping streets were packed, queues everywhere and endless, *gastronoms* suddenly displayed extra heaps of caviar and oranges and wine, and speculation for foreign gifts went crazy. Grandfather Frost, instead of Lenin, was everpresent, and Muscovites sprang through the snow with New Year's trees over their shoulders. As in every country in the world, males worried about money and females worried about new dresses. Those who could reserved tables in the big restaurants, and others arranged parties.

On the big night I had a date with Misha. He had called me from Leningrad—himself—regularly every Sunday, with all traces of anxiety and melancholy gone right from the first. In fact he had entirely forgotten even that there had been cause for fear, and had worked hard for a month saving money for a Moscow spree. I was furious at him for creating such a melodrama for nothing and terrifying me half to death, but there was no point in going on about it because he really didn't know what I meant.

He arrived in a huff nearly three hours late, explaining that

149

at the last moment his newspaper had given him orders to stay where he was, because there was a rumour that another sputnik would go up at midnight and he had been assigned to cover the story. He had had to bribe one of the others to stand by in his place, which had become so involved that it had been necessary to take a plane to get there on time—and that meant he had hardly enough money left for the return fare. 'Who worries, who *worries?* I am HERE!' and he kicked an impromptu *trepak* all over the place.

We joined Kolya and his wife and eight others at the Peking Hotel restaurant. The room was smothered in streamers and decorations, and in the middle stood an immense Christmas tree laden with ornaments. Most of the tree trimmings were like Western ones, but as we passed it I noticed a little silver star with a red hammer and sickle in the middle. I took it, hooliganka again, it was just too good. But nobody could possibly have noticed.

Happy . . . Oh! The happiness was deafening. *Everybody* was intent on getting seriously Russian-drunk that night; by the time we arrived there was already a chaos of song and laughter, with the late-comers pouring vodka into themselves non-stop to catch up. Most of the crowd was young, but there were peasants and officers and everyone, all mixed up with each other, throwing confetti and hugging everyone else. The music was spirited, the dancing frantic—Russian folk tunes, led by a fiddle and an accordion, no jazz, and the dancing was just like something out of old Russia. Waitresses kept dodging pinches and offers of drinks, were finally coaxed or coerced into accepting the drinks, and ended up on the dance floor with everybody else. No one cared about anything, anything, anything, except absolutely letting themselves go and having a concentrated good time. Even though the atmosphere was essentially Russian, I was reminded of something a visiting foreigner had said, which I hadn't understood till then: 'In a crowd anywhere else in the world you feel you are seeing nothing more than an enclave, a minute twig of mankind, compared to this. Here suddenly you are naked—and the whole human race surrounds you. This is the tree: this is humanity!'

Our table was laden with *zakuska*, which was swept away untouched and replaced by fish, also swept away untouched and replaced by chicken, and on and on. Midnight rang out over a loudspeaker, there were anthems and speeches, but no sputnik announcement as we'd thought. 'Aha! You see! For that I nearly didn't get here!' Misha yelled, and opened another bottle of champagne. Pops from other bottles echoed from all corners of the room; Soviet champagne is corked with slippery plastic, and the corks go miles. Everybody tried to hit the chandeliers.

The songs increased in intensity, everyone was competing madly. Pink, green and violet streamers whooshed through the air. Grandfather Frost and his Snow Maiden appeared in person. By 3 a m there wasn't much else to sing, no one left to hug for 1958, and no more champagne, and the generally expressed opinion at our table inclined towards greener pastures. Someone knew about a party.

Outside there wasn't a taxi in sight, and not even a car to thumb a ride from (probably because the one driving rule everyone observes is the one about drunken driving), so we walked through the snow. All was quiet until some home-bound celebrator weaved across our path booming 's NOVIM GODOM!'—Happy New Year—or people leaning out of a brightly lit window waved and shouted to us. The air of friendliness reminded me of the festival—all barriers were down and the whole of the city was one big family party.

The party we were aimed at turned out to be at its peak. American popular songs crooned and blared out of a tape recorder; *Papa Loves Mambo* came on and a few couples were trying to dance it to everyone else's vast amusement. A lot of the men were in a corner angrily denouncing an elderly Romeo who had captured their women—he sat smugly surrounded opposite them, distributing his attentions and looking every inch the great lover in his prime. To break it up someone produced a guitar and began strumming melancholy folk melodies; the group spread itself around on the floor, humming and weaving to the music.

One of the men who had been with us all along was talking to Misha in the kitchen, and when the music stopped and the crowd began to disintegrate I went in to find them. Tolya was the man's name; he spoke excellent English, and switched languages eagerly (everybody wanted practice in speech; many could read, knew the history of English grammar in exact detail, had even had to read *Beowulf* in the original—but couldn't speak). Tolya was a physicist, Misha had told me, and, confidentially, they had originally met three years before when Tolya had been released from . . . he crossed two fingers of one hand over two of the other and looked through them: bars . . . a Leningrad prison and had spent a week in that city before returning to Moscow. Why prison? 'That was in the worst times,' Misha had replied. 'He wrote a poem, rather counter-revolutionary, and a friend who heard it denounced him to the NKVD. It was a very unjust thing, as the police never even saw the poem but sent him away anyway. He was released in an amnesty after 1953. He didn't mean anything serious with the poem, I think, but now he is quite bitter, and has some very strange ideas. He is an anarchist.'

He looked quite ordinary—about forty, with floppy mouse-coloured hair that gradually accumulated in his eyes until he lurched himself backwards to shake it away, a slightly up-turned nose, and a wide Slavic face. His appearance made me think of the saying that after God had made the Russian face he pushed his hand into it to flatten it out.

They were telling jokes.

'Once there was an American going across Siberia in a train,' Tolya began for my benefit. 'As he was passing by one village, the American looked out of the window and saw a lovely girl sunbathing in the grass with no clothes on. He thought she was so beautiful that he married her and took her back to America. About twenty years later the two of them decided to return for a visit to the woman's home. They took the trans-Siberian again, and were soon to get to the village when the conductor came through and shut all the curtains on the windows, even though it was bright daylight. They asked him why, but he wouldn't answer. Finally, after much . . . finagling, so to say, financial dealing, the conductor agreed to explain, and in a whisper he said, "You see, it has been this way for the last twenty years, I don't understand why, but whenever a train comes to this village all the people here come down to the railway line and take off their clothes." '

This went down very well, and an audience accumulated. Misha, with sputniks on the brain, began another.

'Why is the second sputnik different from the earth?'

'Why?'

'Because on one, the dog's life is over, but on the other it continues.'

Tolya laughed, 'Misha! *You!*' then told another.

'One skeleton was walking along the paths of eternity when he met another. "What century are you from?" he asked. "The eleventh," was the reply. They walked along together, as they were going the same way, and soon they met a third skeleton. "What century are you from?" "The sixteenth." A fourth came by then, who said he was from the eighteenth century. The group walked along together for a while, until they met one more skeleton. "What century are *you* from?" they asked him. "You fool," the last answered, "I'm just returning from my night shift." '

It was 5 a m, someone said, and the host was eyeing us in a go-home sort of way. Misha, Tolya and I left together in search of transport. The situation was no better than before, but not a soul in motion; presumably all five million Muscovites had finally collapsed. We three had somehow miraculously been granted second winds, and crunched through the snow happily. Then Misha began wondering about the New Year sputnik, and there was a change of mood.

'I suppose they tried and failed,' Tolya said thoughtfully. 'But of course we shall never know. *Your* country, now,' he directed at me, 'it's all very well for people to laugh at you, but at least everyone knows about it. That side hasn't been mentioned here, of course, but it is quite obvious that if *we* are given such detailed reports on the American . . . um, what is it . . . unsuccess, that your people must be informed.' He sighed. 'Something in the direction of freedom . . .'

'*Nu*, another sputnik story I remember,' he said, to break the silence that had followed his last remarks. 'The sputnik, like everybody else, had to answer a questionnaire for a passport. They asked him all the questions, name, address, occupation, and so on. They then asked him, "Nationality?" and the sputnik replied, "Jew". "Preposterous!" they said. "A fine Russian creation like you, a *Jew*? Why are you a Jew?" "Ah, that is easy to answer," said the sputnik. "Because I wander around the earth and I have nothing." '

No laughter then; Tolya sighed again, 'No, not very funny, is it. But true. Ah yes, very very very true.'

'Are you Jewish?'

'Yes, I am Jewish, I am so Jewish. On questionnaires, anyway. Actually I am the enemy of any religion or nationalism, or any kind of intellectual norms. Faith is evil; it makes men blind—faith in any kind of principle, I mean, not just enthusiasm. That's a fine thing. But yes, I am a Jew, and I cannot even join a library without proclaiming it to the world. Nationality: Jew.'

'This is one of our terrible things,' Misha said angrily. 'Bad, *bad!*'

I had seen how bad it could be. Jews themselves, David and others, had told me. They couldn't have been less Jewish in a religious sense; although some of them had been taught Yiddish by their parents and some expressed curiosity about Israel, most weren't at all interested. Unlike some other countries, actual discrimination went only so far as sometimes barring them from certain key professions—diplomacy and the nuclear sciences—but the general individual attitude of prejudice was often terribly discouraging. Their biggest resentment, however, was that since the three million of them had to be classified a separate nationality and were compelled continually to identify themselves as something apart, they should not be allowed the privileges of a nationality: the Yiddish theatre, literature, newspaper, schools, that had existed before Stalin wiped them out, had not been restored since his death. Freedom of religion, or non-religion, as outlined in the Soviet constitution, seemed to be scrupulously observed, but left the Jewish nationality question entirely out of the picture. As bad as anti-Semitic attitudes can be elsewhere, they seemed to me often worse in Russia. It was a traditional thing, I realized —Russia was the country of the pogrom—but in the context of the present it was hypocritical coming from the same mouths that constantly re-intoned the major criticism of America, discrimination towards Negroes. I could almost never hear a Jew described except with the apologetic preface 'He's a Jew, *but* . . .' (he's very nice, he's very intelligent). And frequent anti-Semitic jokes, Rabinovich this, Rabinovich that (always Rabinovich). Some Russians spent a great deal of their verbal energy on attacking anything and everything Jewish. One woman, whom I dealt with occasionally over my work, was absolutely consumed with loathing, which she rarely stopped venting on everyone in her vicinity, describing such outrages and atrocities perpetrated by that hideous race, in such an hysterical tone, that argument was out of the question. I nodded and ignored it as much as possible. After being submitted to these barrages for month after month, one day I met a good friend of hers, who let it slip that the woman was herself Jewish. I suppose she answered the nationality question 'Russian', and had developed an aggressive shell to stay undiscovered. Whether such a thing is widespread I have no idea, but if so it might explain a great deal.

Tolya felt more resentment than most, but with more cause. He thought that his 'nationality' had had a lot to do with his arrest; he couldn't understand why he should be penalized for something he was so indifferent to; and as a physicist there were difficulties over access to certain material that he needed for his research (although scientists in general were the most free of the intellectuals).

'We can't be trusted, naturally, in strategic areas—we'd go straight off and hand everything over to Israel! We can't be trusted anyway. But you trust me, don't you, Misha?' he patted Misha's back. 'A good boy, Misha.'

We had walked some distance by then without coming across a sign of life, either animate or automotive. A bus would have done if we could have found one, but it was further complicated by the fact that Misha was staying just as far out of the centre as I was, but in the opposite direction. Tolya offered to put us up. 'I live very near here, *Amerikanka* can have the bed and we have plenty of floor. We have a great deal to talk about anyway—there is so much I must hear, and these opportunities are rare.'

His room was incredible. Every surface was littered with ancient cigarette ends, empty vodka bottles and miscellaneous trash, and submerged in books. On the walls, Tolya had hung tremendous sheets of green paper that he used as blackboards and had covered with chalked calculations and formulas. The best was yet to come, though; he opened a cupboard to get some food for us, and it was almost three feet deep in old ends of black bread. He apologized automatically for it all— 'I simply can't be bothered with such things. Terrible, isn't it.' Out of the cupboard emerged half a loaf of relatively new bread and a shrivelled lump of salami. We ate a little and what bread was left seemed destined to join its predecessors in the bottom of the cupboard.

After a colossal fuss the men gallantly bowed their way out of the room and I got into bed, the condition of which was not exactly reassuring but who could complain. After they had returned, installed themselves on the floor, and turned out the light, Tolya sat up abruptly. 'But what is this? We must *talk*,' he said. 'You know my story?'

'Some. It's very interesting—I wanted to talk to *you*.'

Misha mumbled, turned over, and soon gave up the struggle. He started snoring softly.

'The boy is asleep—that is better. Of course he is a wonderful boy, but things are difficult, you know. My best friend once denounced me to the secret police, and it is harder to get over these things.'

'Misha told me a little about it. What happened? Or shouldn't I ask?'

'Of course, of course, *nichevo*. It is done, and you're all right anyway. Just 58-10, you know.'

'58-10 what?'

'Article 58 of the Soviet constitution,' he recited, 'is for counter-revolutionaries. Section 10 is for anti-Soviet propaganda.'

'You wrote a poem?'

He laughed. 'Ah, yes, and it is not bad, either, my poem. Nothing like our friend Misha's poetry—he is a genius, you know. Mine was quite childish of me really, but it has all been worthwhile in the end. I fooled them, you see, because even prison is not so bad for someone like me. They couldn't take away what mattered—thoughts cannot be in prison, and I had many years to think. Some of my best work was done during those years; I made some quite important calculations that I have used ever since in my research. And I learned English—or otherwise this would never be. Also German and French, so I can read foreign material now even before it is translated. Probably nothing of the sort would have happened if I had gone on as before, and my whole life would have been wasted. But the poem, yes, that would amuse you I think. It was based on *The Raven* by Edgar Allan Poe—not all translatable, but you know where it is: "Suddenly there came a tapping, as of someone gently rapping, rapping at my chamber door . . ." I made this rapping the secret police, in the night and everything, it was very obvious. Most obvious, because the raven was the raven indeed—raven is Russian slang for black maria. It was quite a success, my poem, I hear that it has since been a favourite of political prisoners! But there aren't so many now, of course, there are no more forced-labour camps: the ravens are appeased.'

'What do *you* think about things getting better?' I asked him, remembering what Shura had said. 'I've heard many reasons. One is that everyone with guts or rebelliousness or intelligence has already been arrested and there isn't anyone left . . .'

'No,' he broke in, 'many have been released, and in any case new ones spring up all the time.'

'Because there is more caution, then, that's another one.'

'No, there is less if anything.'

'Then because it's genuinely more free?'

'Undoubtedly it is. But not sufficiently so. There was a noticeable increase of freedom after Stalin, but a lot of things were clamped down again after Hungary. The main thing is that there are so few guarantees that what freedom we have will remain. You really cannot predict what may happen here, even in two days. Maybe it will be all right, I don't know. We have a far greater chance now, after Stalin's crimes were exposed. It would be very difficult indeed for them to try all that again.'

'Are you really an anarchist?'

'*Da, ya anarkeest.*' He tried to cackle wickedly.

'What do you believe?'

'Oh what you want to know! How will I learn anything from you like this?'

'Please? Please please please?'

'All right. If you promise to answer *me* later.'

'Of course.'

'Well, what then?'

'Communism?'

'I think that communism is a basically foolish conception, very nice, but unsound. It is impossible because its basic premises are wrong. Its origins are understandable: it was imagined by men, themselves in capitalistic societies, where all evils spring from economic grounds, and they thought, I suppose, that by correcting this evil *all* evil would disappear. But the theory that man can be given a paradise simply by the regulation of his economy is nonsense. The fundamental Marxist theories behind it, that political and social conditions are a superstructure on an economic base, and that economic factors alone govern history, are wrong. And in any case, within that, that conditions for the workers under capitalism would inevitably get worse—that is also wrong, as we see. Conditions have improved for them—though it is true that their voice is less and less effective—and they do not know it, that is the tragedy. They think they have a real democratic voice, but they are controlled completely.

'Another thing that is wrong with the Marxist predictions here—the withering away of the state, which of course would lead to my anarchism, shows no signs of doing so and nothing has withered. But perhaps it will, and I will happily be proven mistaken.

'Of course we must try all these things out, but I believe we will evolve towards anarchy in the end. I am not naïve enough to suppose that anarchy could work now, but on the whole I think it will solve most problems finally.

'Now an anarchic revolution is improbable because there exist opportunities for demagogy. Men feel that they need an authority, they always want a power greater than themselves. Faith in something is necessary to them for action. This is the sort of faith that I meant before, that I believe is wrong and dangerous. Then, you always have men eager to exploit man's desire for a faith. If an anarchic group were to seize power it could possibly be no more than a new variant of Stalinism, the way people are now. In the name of no power the anarchists could take absolute power.

'Education is necessary, awareness must be built up in the masses.'

'But how long would this take?'

'I don't know, I don't believe in prophecies or guesses. It may not be possible for centuries, but man's progress is unreliable—it may speed up tremendously or stop altogether. There is no way of knowing.'

'What then, in the meantime?'

'As far as the present is concerned, here, democracy must be restored. Citizenship must be free, not obligatory. Freedom of conviction must be absolute, and freedom of speech nearly so.'

'Nearly so?'

'Oh, espionage, various cases where a word is a crime. It cannot be absolute for some time.'

'And what about the economy?'

'For the Soviet Union, changes of the economic system can wait, they are not the essential thing at present. What is important now are radical political changes. I cannot go further than that, either in relation to this country or others which I know nothing about.

'It would take weeks to tell you everything. Anyway, I am a scientist, not a political thinker, and my words are unimportant. Please, you have many to talk to but I have no one—I want you to explain certain things. It is difficult sifting facts here, you know; I get both sides of it (he patted the radio beside him) but there is no agreement about *anything*. Quite in-cr-r-redible.'

I answered his questions, as many as I could. Soon the early morning light began to creep in, making the room look weirder than ever; unidentifiable shapes and toppling stacks of books shed eerie shadows on the walls. Misha never woke, and soon neither of us was awake enough to carry on either. The sun came up: we went to sleep.

Late in the afternoon I came to. January 1st, 1958. Tolya wasn't there, but Misha didn't seem to have moved since my last vision of him. Things were moving in circles, it occurred to me then, remembering Elenagorsk. I got up and went in search of our host.

He was tracked down in the kitchen, after a series of rather unfortunate collisions with the neighbours in the dark corridor. There was a middle-aged woman pottering over the stove, and Tolya, his eyes full of straggling hair, was dealing with something on the table. 'Good morning' *'s novim godom'*, etc.

'Does she speak English?' I asked him, automatically anxious.

'No, it's all right. Actually, I had to tell the others that there was a foreign Communist staying with me—doing research on Soviet living conditions. I couldn't think of a thing.' He slowly took in my rather unresearcher-like appearance. I had on both the party dress and greenish tinge from the night before.

'Do I look the part?' I asked hopefully.

'Um, well, not . . . exactly. *Nichevo, nichevo.* This is Natalya Alexandrovna,' he introduced the woman, who had been nearly killing herself trying to look at me through the back of her head. 'She is my good friend and ally, she worries about me . . .' he smiled at her charmingly and she blushed. Then she remembered that it was all right to look at me now, and turned abruptly. Her face seemed to be in two halves; her fascinated solemn wide eyes had no relation to the broad grin below them. She looked about fifty, round, pink, and pleasant. The eyes followed me as I washed in the sink—the bathroom hadn't been functioning for some years now, Tolya explained: there was something wrong with the plumbing or something. Since they lived on the sixth floor of an apartment house on top of a hill, the pressure sometimes failed and they had to keep the bathroom sink and bath full of water to use when it did. It occurred to me a moment later that I must be quite Sovietized not to have even thought of asking why the plumbing hadn't been fixed—I had accepted it with as much resignation as Tolya.

Tolya had somehow unearthed a new loaf of bread and some cheese, and was making a valiant but helpless effort to make it all very civilized. Natalya Alexandrovna took over masterfully. 'She likes to do it, so I let her do it,' Tolya shrugged. 'She would like most to get her hands on my room, but you know how impossible it is to concentrate when everything is organized, and . . . besides, once these women . . .' he didn't finish, but looked at Natalya Alexandrovna again, who blushed again. She made us tea and sat down with us, drinking hers the old Russian way, through a lump of sugar. Until her curiosity was satisfied she continued to stare, like a child or any natural human being who hasn't been taught that it's peculiar to stare. All Russians had for me a little of that quality. They haven't been exposed to Etiquette and brittle sophistication, and the result is this disarming honesty and realness that sometimes made me feel ashamed of the more unnecessary niceties created by Western civilization.

I asked Tolya a little about Natalya Alexandrovna—since I didn't know her and she was older than me, I had to use the respectful patronymic however much of a mouthful it was. She was overjoyed to be talked about, and her face became one again, all smiling.

'She is forty-three, a widow,' Tolya said. 'Her husband died in the war and left her with two young children. She teaches in a children's garden, and now one of her sons is old enough to work too. The other one is her pride—he will be a very good pianist some day. He studies at the Conservatoire.'

She understood 'conservatoire', and smiled harder than ever. Then she asked Tolya if I would like to ask her questions. I don't think she had often been the focus of so much attention and interest, and she couldn't quite decide whether to beam with pride, gaze at Tolya rapturously, or examine my shoes.

I asked her what she wanted most. She gave it some thought, then arrived at a three-part answer: a flat; better material conditions—higher wages, lower prices; and to be able to visit Miami, America.

'Miami?'

'She has a cousin in this Miami. She thinks it would be nice—she hears from him sometimes.'

I asked Tolya the same question then.

'Freedom of communication—with people—is most important, I think. Just like this, *Amerikanka i Russki*. Or better, no Americans, no Russians, simply people: all the same.

'Then the second ... freedom of communciation with *ideas*. I must know everyone's ideas, I must be free to read everything, and understand what all people are thinking. In my work and in general. The third, travel. I don't know what more—the material life is not of such importance to me. Really what I would like is just what you have. That would be a beginning, anyway.'

We went back to Natalya Alexandrovna. Her wages were 500 roubles a month, 430 clear. She seemed pretty fatalistic about possibilities of material improvement; her life had been nothing but dreadful struggle to support herself and her children, and the struggle remained the same. It was only beginning to ease up now because her son Igor was working. But even so, she had no time for relaxation even if there were opportunities to do the things she wanted. Her daily life consisted of getting to work early and running races with young children all day, coming home exhausted and then having to cook and clean, then in her time away from work (Saturday afternoons and Sundays), shopping for the next week, mending and laundry, going to the public baths, and sleeping if she could. She detested the sputniks and everything they represented, and only wanted a little rest and pleasure sometime in her life. The sputniks, she felt, were directly responsible for depriving her of these things. Her grin left her entirely at the very mention of the word 'sputnik'; it seemed as if all her years of pent-up fury had been released on them.

She said she knew no one who had no complaints. (What about Communist Party members? The ones in superior positions naturally feel communism is good—it is communism indeed for them. The others are opportunists.) No one she knew admired anyone in the government, and they loathed that fat peasant. But Malenkov, now. A dreamy smile came into her eyes. Under him, things had got better; prices went down and there were more things in the shops. But since Malenkov things had changed so slowly. Perhaps now, though . . . 1958.

'Is she religious?'

'Yes, a little, but I try to talk her out of such nonsense.'

'What does she think about freedom?'

'Oh, I can tell you that without asking her. She doesn't

think about it, she doesn't have any idea what it is. She hasn't seen it, heard about it, it is nothing but an abstract concept that she could never grasp, and even now she believes that the Soviet Union has the greatest amount of democracy, and that the West is certainly as bad, if not worse. It's funny, with people like her. She resents all of "them", the top people, and is determined not to believe anything "they" tell her, yet it is obvious that propaganda has effect if it is repeated often enough. For instance, she believes that all the peoples in the capitalist countries are exploited. But she knows that their lives are better, from what she has seen. I have argued with her about this, but she cannot see any contradictions. She keeps saying, "Yes, but I *know* that the masses are oppressed." But, as you can see, I have talked her out of some of her apathy. She used to feel nothing but inertia, and think only in terms of day-to-day problems; now she relates some of them to causes. Seeing the festival helped, too, and she sometimes believes the letters her cousin sends her. The speech of Khrushchev at the Twentieth Congress as well. Of course she never heard the whole speech, but much of the information in it reached her, and she was frightfully disturbed. All that faith before—but it was lies! What could she *ever* believe again? Now she was forced to consider, to weigh, to examine these people and these situations, decide about them herself. She won't simply accept all that tripe anymore.

'Ah, Natasha, you are learning to *think*, no?' he leaned over and smiled at her.

'S *novim godom*.' A creaking, semi-conscious Misha shambled into the room.

14

American Pickles and the Russian Character

SOMETIMES MOSCOW SEEMED to be the centre of the real universe instead of a universe in itself. Elements from everywhere, disproportionate but representing almost every idea and way of life, came together there more frequently, or at least more noticeably, than anywhere else, making the city something like an over-crowded summit conference. Or perhaps a conference absorbed in something more significant, I sometimes thought—the fate of mankind.

That week I went with a foreign newspaperman to one of those embassy cocktail parties, given by the Burmese, who were celebrating some national day or other. The blocks outside were lined for acres around with long black diplomatic cars, and a heavy concentration of militiamen were stationed at regular intervals all along the surrounding streets. Inside: buffets laden with food and drink, and from the array of national plumage, something of the atmosphere of a costume ball. The views of the guests differed almost as much as their origins. There was Bulganin exchanging toasts with the Burmese ambassador. There was Mikoyan, there the American ambassador; or an English Communist and an English Tory journalist, in some ways a more interesting contrast. Top officials, visiting VIPS from everywhere, and so on in their lesser numbers down to third secretaries and French tourists. All blended together into the very core of the world's problem, hardly

165

diluted. And hardly existing, judging from the friendship on all sides. None met on a battlefield: this was no-man's-land, where the scores and terms were equal. They were individuals representing themselves, not just representing countries, and so they were tolerant of each other. There were no problems or misunderstandings, no disagreements or snubs or hostilities, no difficulties over semantics.

I stood alone on the edge for a moment, looking at the little world. What's the matter with the big world? Are people so narrow that they can't project this into everything else? It's all so easy! I felt like shouting—*Look* at yourselves! You all *like* each other! You're all the *same!* All you have to do is be as understanding and civilized in the name of your nation as you are as individuals!

But no. Oversimplifying, someone would have said. (My favourite word.) What corn, another. Madness, nonsense, ridiculous, absurd. So I walked up to the end of the room to have a closer look at Bulganin.

There were three types of Westerners in Moscow, and the total number was minute enough to make them conspicuous and interesting. Every individual had a distinct status, upon which depended his relative privileges and his relations with Russians. There were the temporary tourists and delegations, all quite insulated from the exciting best and the depressing worst of the city they were in. They got piled in and out of their hotels into buses and big black cars, shepherded through the Agricultural Exhibition, the Bolshoi, the university, the mausoleum, a *kolkhoz*, a factory, a museum, never catching breath or able to see, and shunted off again on a jet that flies no faster than the speed they felt all along.

The other two groups were the sympathizing residents-for-life, and the semi-permanent diplomats and journalists. They all had advantages—news of the outside world was the main one, but materially life was better for them too, all the way to those whose contact with Soviet life was nil, or at least well-cushioned, by their existence in imported chunks of home.

I was as apart from the last group as they were from Russia until I met some Cingalese who invited me to a party. They lived across the courtyard from me in a big apartment house entirely reserved for official foreigners. This meant more space, an elevator that didn't stop at night and went down, and militiamen at each door to keep Russians away. All foreign embassies were so guarded, but I hadn't known it went so far. Going to the party, I crossed the court, but when I reached the door the militiaman proved finally that I really could look Russian—he wouldn't let me in. He wanted to know my name, where I lived, whom was I going to see, which apartment did they live in, what was their nationality and what was mine, why didn't I have a passport with me, and the rest of my life's history. Not that any of my answers mattered, because he wouldn't let me in anyway. Somewhere along the line I had told him I was born in Hollywood, and that clinched it. Nothing further would bring him to believe that I wasn't a faking Russian. But it made me so mad—not that he wouldn't believe me, but the fact that you had to be screened before going to a perfectly innocent party—that I went on talking to him anyway, joking, threatening, pleading, shouting, cajoling, anything to find a way around. I could have gone home for my identification documents, which had been issued to me by then, but that would have been defeat. A similar kind of defeat came anyway in the end; one of the Cingalese happened to come out, and he interceded. He said he hadn't experienced that one before, but life was like that and he wasn't surprised.

Upstairs, the apartment was filled with very beautiful Swedish furniture; Spanish sherry, Scotch whisky, French cognac, and American vodka; American, French, Cingalese and Tamil music; English cigarettes, Cingalese food, and saried women. The combination was pretty odd, but if I had been led in blindfolded I never would have dreamed it was Russia. We ate hot gooey things on rice with our fingers, a few of them danced wildly, others reminisced about sun and palm trees, then everyone decided they wanted to go to see *War and Peace*, which was playing at the American Club.

I didn't know about the club and was fascinated to see what it could be like. Fear at the reception I might receive inside, and the thought of more militiamen to face outside—rather tougher ones who wouldn't be likely to mistake me for a Cingalese—made me hesitate. But I wanted to go enough to be persuaded.

Diplomatic immunity, or something, got me past the militiamen, and inside no one bothered at all about anyone. In any case, the atmosphere was such a knockout blow to me that I forgot at once. A juke-box! Playing the latest Perry Como. A lot of crewcuts, and shininess, and drawly accents. At the bar some men in draped sports jackets sipping highballs, and behind it a real American bartender, specially imported. The only, quite unintentional, Russian touch was *War and Peace*, and even that bore little resemblance to anything except America.

I learned more about the people there as time went on. The Moscow Americans had a tough time, to a large extent self-inflicted, and probably led the most neurotic existence there ever has been or could be. To begin with they lived in America, their own little faraway piece, and no mistake about that. The British diplomats, by way of contrast, learned Russian as a rule and were encouraged to meet Muscovites in a friendly way, but the Americans didn't want to, weren't permitted to, and didn't try. For all of the employees at the embassy except the top ones, Moscow was a 'hardship post' that they volunteered for, weren't assigned to, and there were appropriate compensations, extra allowances and pay, to make up for the hardship. They were there for two years each, but were permitted to leave after one, and according to statistics often gave up even before that. Apparently the rate of nervous breakdowns was shattering. I forgot to ask if they brought their own psychiatrist.

They could never talk about anything, as all their buildings were either wired or suspected of being wired, and they didn't leave their buildings. There was a kind of geiger-counter

gadget that found microphones, or something like that, anyway they had an idea where they were located. Mainly they
had been found in bathrooms and bedrooms, I was told, but
one was even discovered right above the ambassador's desk
in the United States crest, concealed among the olive
branches. It wasn't removed, none of them were; the procedure was to leave them alone but knowing their where-
abouts not to give them anything. If necessary, people could
always write notes to each other.

Not only could they never talk about anything, but they
would never talk to anyone either. They very rarely met Russians, and almost never made friends with them. They weren't
permitted to travel out of a twenty-five-mile radius around
Moscow (nor Soviet diplomats out of Washington). Such
was the closedness of it all that even Russian food was suspect; at any rate, all food was flown in. The British on the
other hand bought most of their supplies locally, and the
chef was talented at judging the market. If cabbages came on
sale, he bought thousands at one go and stored them in deep
freezes, on the assumption that next week there probably
wouldn't be any more cabbages.

I met some American correspondents who led similar lives.
As journalists, the men had some contact with the Soviet
world—but not much, because their news sources were mainly
official Tass releases, what scraps could be culled from the
Moscow newspapers, or the occasional speech or embassy
function; all news was censored going out so no results from
undercover research could accomplish anything. The official
line was 'censorship does not exist'; to uphold this illusion
the censors were concealed behind a wall, and the editing was
described as 'improvement of style'. It is worth mentioning
that such censorship has been an eternal thing in Russia,
and existed long before 1917. Journalists submitted their
stories on one side of the wall, they came out again blue-
pencilled and style-improved, and the journalist signed something at the bottom to the effect that all corrections were his.
This wasn't quite as sinister and hypocritical as it seemed; I

was told that it was for the benefit of the telegraph office, and that such a regulation exists throughout Europe. Just what would be blue-pencilled was never quite clear, and the correspondents spent half their time trying to figure out what would or wouldn't get past. When the price of vodka increased on New Year's day, one newspaperman filed: 'There was bad news for the man in the street today—the price of vodka rose five roubles.' It came out of the wall 'The price of vodka rose five roubles.'

Many of them went there with the idea of interviewing Khrushchev, or at least talking to him. This was tricky, and if official permission wasn't granted the only opportunity for a fling was an embassy reception. Then the job was to get an invitation to the reception. The procedure was to ring up the embassy giving the party, ask for the ambassador or the first secretary, congratulate him on the occasion, and somehow keep on talking until, in desperation, he invited you.

It was difficult enough simply to receive permission to stay in Moscow at all; the journalists had one of those unbackfireable circular jobs to tackle. They could not send stories until they were accredited, they were told. They could not be accredited until they were residents, they were then told. Finally they could not be granted permission to reside until they were accredited to send stories. All of it was blackly confusing to Westerners who had never encountered such reasoning. I had full sympathy for their difficulties, but never for their, and their families', lack of attempts at ordinary friendliness, or at least interest, in Moscow. Even going for a walk seemed to be an unheard-of thing. They stayed within their self-contained luxurious community, so ingrown that they were all intricately wound up in each other's daily existence. Taking no part in the life around them, they lived in apartments that could easily have been mistaken for displaced Park Avenue, where they gossiped and played bridge and bingo and drank too much, there in one of the most exciting cities in the world.

I watched them once in one of their homes, and couldn't evade the sensation of goldfish bowls. I should have been participating, but was too dazed to do anything but mechanically eat my hot dog and potato salad. There were boxes of Kleenex in every room, wall-to-wall carpets, an enormous refrigerator full of Schlitz beer and Coca-Cola, a kitchen with at least one of every single gadget ever invented and crammed to the ceilings with American food. There was even a stock of American dill pickles—no one makes pickles better than the Russians. It seemed the most dreamlike dream I could remember, until they produced some powdered cream to put in the powdered coffee. This added refinement was past my time, and on top of the other, more familiar objects around the place, suddenly made me feel almost faint. If this was the advance of civilization, I felt I'd like to join those of my friends who think they were born in the wrong age. Then I had visions of all the desperately poor, degradingly poor people I had seen in the past months, and I thought how grateful these people should be not to have seen them, not to be disturbed at the thought that all life wasn't this. But then their complacency made me angry. And finally sorry-for-myself, because I couldn't be complacent, ever again.

I knew though that I couldn't put all the blame on them for their isolation. A foreigner's relations with Russians are a long struggle between fear and curiosity. In my case, curiosity had always been able to win, but fear was everywhere, and one had to assume that it represented something. But for me, as time went on, I could only increasingly think that it was more hollow than real. Nothing had happened to Misha—and he had been so *sure*. So had all my other friends, the ones who looked under all the beds and poked in all the holes to find Them or It, and the whole assortment of imaginary spies, detectives, letter-openers, telephone-listeners. Sooner or later, when nothing came of any of it, I just settled back in my seat for the inevitable cloak-and-dagger grade C it all was, humouring them and not believing. So I went through all the silly Russian-disguises, and the conversations that could only be had on the street, and the racing around in and out of taxis and buses to evade the little man who wasn't there. How could he have been there? I attributed the fear to left-over Stalinism, though in whatever situation it seemed frantically unlikely in the gigantic proportions described, if only because of the sheer manpower problem. If the 'organization' was as enormous as all that, there would be so many people involved that how could anything be kept secret? There wouldn't be room enough to store all those daily millions of files and tapes. And if it were true, for instance, that at the Metropole there were microphones in every corner room and every room ending in 25—who could listen to the 24-hour results, anyhow? Finally, never having found much interest in efficiency in any other area, I couldn't picture it suddenly being displayed here. They would have had to be extraordinarily efficient to succeed in leaving no evidence of any kind even of their existence. And there was no evidence. I never felt any shortage of counter-revolutionary characters, intellectual or crackpot, in my vicinity, but nothing ever happened to anyone, either for their beliefs or for telling me about them (which they seemed to feel was worse).

Then I met one more correspondent, a European who made an effort to get out into the city and understand it. I often saw him in the places where Russians go. Once he explained to me what official foreigners had to fear, and where I was wrong.

'When I had been here for three months,' he began, 'I came to the conclusion that it was the easiest place in the world to make friends. The Russians I met were so incredibly warm to me, and hospitable!' I nodded in agreement—that was what I felt. Then he went on. 'But after six months I knew it was the most difficult. People just disappeared. I made friends with someone, saw him perhaps two or three times, everything going splendidly, then I never heard from him again. This happened with everyone—it was fantastic— and I had no idea why. For weeks I lived through agonies, without being able to find out what had happened to them. Then once, in Red Square, I met one of my friends again. He behaved very strangely, kept trying to run off, apologize and then go. I had to stop him; I had to know. He said that when we had been together last we had been followed, and that afterwards they had brought him to a police station and warned him never to see me again. He said all this very quickly, looking about to see if anyone were watching, then, "I'm sorry, I must go now. Good luck." And he disappeared in the crowd.

'Somehow it still seemed unreal to me. Like you. One reads about such things—but happening? Really? I simply couldn't believe it, even though I thought I'd known completely what to expect. It was a nightmare! But . . . the next time, I watched. I had to understand.

'I met two young university students—they intercepted me outside the hotel asking for dollars or foreign clothes. I told them that I wasn't a tourist and had nothing, but they walked along with me and we became friendly. They invited me to a party a friend of theirs was giving, and we arranged to meet the next evening in a crowded place so we wouldn't be noticed. We did, and then went all around the city before our final destination—you know how it goes. The party was good, we danced and sang and drank quite a lot—toasts to this and that—nothing at all political. They weren't politically minded, just having a good time. It ended quite late, and the three of us decided to share a taxi. The streets were empty, but right outside the house were two of those black limousines, looking very conspicuous. We found a taxi, drove off, and I looked back through the window: the two cars were following. First we went to one boy's home and dropped him off. When we started up again, I noticed that only one of the cars was behind us. At my hotel, I got out and so did the other boy—he lived nearby. I paid the bill, said goodnight, and went inside the door, but I stayed there and watched. The other car had stopped behind the taxi, and after I was out of sight two men got out and went up to the boy. They took him with them.

'I haven't seen either of them since, and don't expect to. Nor can I possibly meet anyone else. It's not just a nightmare now, not a dream anymore.'

The story astonished me, but answered many questions. It

had been another one of those times when the answers were difficult to find because of the generally schizophrenic state of things. We love foreigners, we hate foreigners; we trust them, we don't; we are free, we are not; everyone is a spy, no one is. Who knows? I did know, later, that if this particular injustice applied to me to any degree, my complaints had to be aimed in more than one direction. Somebody who shouldn't have done so told me something I should have realized but didn't: that the Americans knew what I was up to in as much detail as anyone else. Not only had they been fully aware of my visit to the American Club, and many of my other movements, but they were staggeringly well acquainted with my whole life's history, past and present.

Members of the foreign 'colony', permanent residents, have neither material privileges nor social penalties to the same extent as the official people. Some of them, having kept their native citizenship, live in relative comfort from what they can import, but many are Soviet naturalized and have the same problems as natives. Whatever their motives or backgrounds, many were inspiring examples of people who had given their lives for an ideal and suffered for it. One man I knew who, like Giuseppe, had spent many exiled years inside the Arctic Circle mining coal, and whose life had been a whole series of tragedies, still had enthusiasm and faith that could have stood up to anyone's. Lenin's 'You can't make an omelette without breaking eggs' excused a multitude of sins, even those affecting him. They would never happen again. The Soviets had many obstacles to overcome that deserved sympathy.

As another foreigner, and one who could explain things in an outsider's frame of reference, he was trying one day to tell me about the Russian character and how much it had to do with the success or failure of the experiment. He said that the traditional man, the one everyone knows so well from Russia's literature—indolent, stubborn, submissive, sometimes cruel and corrupt—is one of the biggest impediments to the Soviet dream, and something that gets no mention, certainly no understanding, from Western critics.

'They're *small*-minded, the Russians, incredibly small-minded, for one thing. You know, it's not even a century since they were serfs, and often they're still serfs in their attitudes. They have absolutely no sense of the collective idea, and that's some problem in a socialist country.

'Things like this have happened to show me: during the war I was collecting wool for wounded soldiers. It was inevitably the same; I'd go into one house and the woman would weep—such histrionics!—and no wool, says she. Then I'd go next door and the same thing all over again, all the stops out, no wool, but the woman would say, "I just saw you coming out of Anna Ivanovna's house—you know she has wool, she's hidden it under the bed. She's lying, that Anna Ivanovna, if she tells you she has none!"

'Or another example. I was working in a factory once, and I used to take a thermos of tea with me every day to drink during breaks. I'd put it down while I worked, and come back later to find the thermos almost empty. All the workers would act as if they had no idea what I was talking about if I asked them who had drunk the tea. This happened every day, and every day they had blank faces. Then I had an idea, and suggested to them that it would be nice if each of us contributed ten kopecks a day and bought tea for the group. They were aghast! "Why should we want tea?" they all said. "*We* don't want any old tea," and so on.

'This collective idea thing. A boss can yell at a worker for any reason, or for no reason, just to vent his spleen, but not a soul will come to the worker's defence. In the Western countries nothing like that could happen, the others wouldn't stand for it, but here the most they would do is take the worker aside individually later and sympathize with him—"He shouldn't say things like that to you!" they say, a fat lot of good that does, but they'd never for a minute think of going to the boss and accusing him of wronging someone.

'The Zhukov affair turned out much the same way. When Zhukov was ousted—well, you could never imagine how popu-

lar he was. Everybody loved him. Yet of the soldiers who had
fought by his side in the war, who worshipped him and his
military genius, not one would step forward to defend him.

'So many things of that sort happen to make others condemn us, but none of them understand that many of the
things that are wrong are *Russian* and not *Soviet*. The way
Russians are habitually dissatisfied, for instance, the way they
grumble and groan but never lift a hand to help. They complain to a degree that would mean insurrection in the West,
but here it means nothing. Yet the paradox of the Russian
character comes out when you consider the self-sacrifice and
united effort they are capable of when their country is threatened. But foreigners meet them and draw the wrong conclusions, almost invariably—they come here and condemn
socialism outright when they meet a few grumblers and make
deductions from them. They don't understand that despite
these few who seem to indicate that the system can't work—
it *is* working!

'That's a funny character trait, this self-ridicule. A Russian
may call himself a fool over and over again—"Oh, what
wonderful clothes you have" they may tell you, or "Oh, what
a beautiful cigarette lighter". "We could never do anything like
that here, we're no good"—but! Just *you* once try calling him
a fool, and you won't be left standing on your feet. He can
criticize himself, but no one else is permitted to. Foreigners
rarely get past that though, they never discover the real power
and pride of the Russian. His pride is underneath, buried
but strong.

'A Russian's patriotism is an unusual thing. In England
they have a patriotism based on tradition, in America a
patriotism of freedom, but here it's of the earth. There again,
the serf aspect. Everything in their behaviour and speech is
earthy. They never ask a stranger just "Where do you come
from?" or "What city do you come from?" they say "What
zemlya, what land are you from?" All the people, except these
few city ones, know how to milk a cow, how to mow with a
scythe, how to ride. They love horses—they look at a beautiful

car with curiosity, but at a beautiful horse with admiration.

'I always remember a soldier—I saw him on his deathbed in the war. He was delirious, and kept shouting "My windmill! I won't let the Germans take my windmill!" He wasn't thinking of Stalin or dying for that moustached monster, like they tell you—he wanted his land and the windmill where he ground his corn. That kind of nationalism is much more valuable in the long run.

'There are other things that tie in with this Russian thing too. It was ironic, really, that socialism should come first to this country, just about the least socialist in outlook, the last place where anyone would have imagined success. And now, the things the West despises most about us they really believe are direct results of *socialism* here. The Iron Curtain—somehow outsiders believe that this curtain was a Soviet invention. In fact, Russia was always isolated as much as it is today, except for a privileged few. The whole question of lack of contact, and other things too, such as some civil liberties which are less important in this context, and missing now—fill Westerners with such indignation. These rights are as necessary as air to Westerners, they are their tradition, their birthright—their patriotism. They *are* necessary, I'm not denying that, and they'll come—I promise you! But up to now none, not one, of these things has *ever existed* here. The secret police were created by Ivan the Terrible, and the whole atmosphere of secrecy and mystery has been flourishing here for centuries; this again is Russian, not Soviet, and it has nothing to do with socialism. You cannot condemn socialism because of Russian failings.

'It's a difficult job to change human nature, but it's not impossible, and it will work here when people have more education. It's already gone a long way. You might think Russia was filled with socialist heroes from reading our papers. It isn't, of course, but there are more of them all the time. The spirit will capture everyone when they understand—the spirit of a country growing, where the future is coming, then all at once it's here.'

Why should I not speak to you?

MISHA STAYED IN MOSCOW for a few more days. When he left it was goodbye, because I was leaving soon. I jokingly offered to marry him—in name only—if he liked, so he could leave with me and go to his island in the ocean, but he graciously declined. 'That was a moment of weakness,' he said, '—that talk about the island. Of course it is my dream still, but it will stay where it is and I will get there someday soon. I will come to see you someday soon too, but I can never desert my country that I love. Anything that is wrong I must work to finish, everything that is new I must work to find. I must help the others—to work for communism.' He laughed when he said that, but he meant it.

I made the same offer to Shura, who hated so much. He also declined. He had to work too, he said, for the revolution.

Then I tried Sergei. He said he'd absolutely love to, so at least the personal rejection element was cut down to a minimum. He did some research into the matter, but showed up defeated and dejected one day. 'I cannot, I cannot, oh! such a pity,' he wailed. He said it didn't work that way. If a foreign man married a Soviet girl he could get her out, but a Soviet man was not permitted to leave with a foreign wife. Some equality of the sexes that turned out to be!

What happened to the others? Nothing, really, everything is just the same with them, and that's why this is such a mess of a story. Or not just the same, because now nothing there is the same as it was then. They are all involved in their country's rumbling and groaning: muttering or fighting it, accepting or encouraging it.

David has still not got a *propiska*, and no one is bothering him. Boris, the painter, has become quite a success, and some of Misha's poetry has been published. There was not a dry eye in the house at the premier of *The Memory of the Heart*: even Khrushchev, so the reports go, wept with emotion. The metro station outside my window, the one that never seemed to get anywhere, has got somewhere, and will open soon. Dunya has died, and with her a further small part of the church.

And there were more people—there were all kinds. I never saw a collective farm, a factory, or even the mausoleum. People were the main thing, and their reactions to their world.

There were non-Muscovites. A man from Yakut—a huge, primitive, completely isolated region in the far north. He looked a little like an Eskimo, and he was the first Yakutian who had ever learned English; he was in Moscow translating textbooks so that other Yakutians could follow his example. A Jew from Vilnius, who came to Moscow now and then to keep up-to-date with cultural developments. He went to the ballet, theatre, and art exhibitions and tore around seeing people in the most breath-takingly concentrated way, storing up for another six months. He explained that the chief problem in Lithuania was that the Lithuanians hated the Russians, Poles, Estonians, Latvians, and Jews; the Jews hated the Lithuanians, Poles, Latvians, Estonians, and Russians; and the Russians really didn't care much one way or the other. I think it was even more complicated than that, but I can't remember the subtleties. Anyway, the driving force around there, he said, consisted of doing in as many of The Others, whomever they might be, as one could.

The most politically aloof creature I met was a young

woman who was so out of this world that she was hardly more than dimly aware of the existence of a man named Khrushchev on top somewhere, and that there had once been a character named Marx; it never became apparent that she was conscious of any of the mechanisms controlling her existence. That is not easy in Russia. Her interest was poetry. She was particularly keen on Dylan Thomas, and spent most of her time digging out what she could at the Lenin Library. The trouble was that though she could recite everything by heart she wasn't always sure what he had in mind, and I found myself continually being cornered to explain his more obscure allusions. Neither of us was very impressed by my success.

And the most politically conscious. There were Communists, as dedicated as priests. They were willing to stand by discipline to the end, sacrifice themselves, work infinitely hard. 'I love the Party,' one of them said, with such *fervour*, 'and I love my country. For many years I was too selfish and self-interested to be worthy of membership, and it was a long time before I realized what was important. Until I reached the stage of being willing to give even my life for my beliefs, I was not ready. Now I work hard, yes, and by doing it I am personally happy and fulfilled, but that is not important. I am helping my country and my people, and I am helping to change the world!' He had a nice car and flat, too, but only his family got pleasure out of them. His children were promising *stiliagi* candidates.

There were more people who had been imprisoned. When I met one and the subject was mentioned I usually steered clear, assuming that it had been for political reasons and the same old thing. That always was the case until I met a very heroic figure who had actually been in jail for embezzlement. He was suffering still; having been expelled from the Party, he had incurred the gravest, most degrading stigma of all. But he was philosophical about it, didn't blame anyone in the slightest, and was absolutely loyal.

There were Names. Guy Burgess at the ballet one night. He seemed pleasant. My boss at the publishing house, who had been Stalin's interpreter at Tehran, Yalta, and Potsdam. He was working on a translation of *Roosevelt and Hopkins*, and now and then asked me to help him with difficult idioms. He had known all the people involved, and sometimes would tell me amusing, harmless little anecdotes about the habits and mannerisms of the Very Important People we came across in the text. I met many dancers from the Bolshoi. Except for the stars, they were rather poorly paid, both in relation to other artistic fields and to the prestige they commanded. Apparently members of the Bolshoi orchestra made far more. Stalin, the story goes, attended a performance there once and was shocked by the low level of artistry among the musicians. He asked one of them why they couldn't do better, and the reply was that they didn't get paid enough. He promptly ordered that their salaries should be doubled. But the dancers have always been too good to rate such attention. Among the male dancers, incidentally, were the only homosexuals I heard of among all Russians. No one ever discussed homosexuality, but prudery wasn't the reason; it isn't a problem, and virtually doesn't exist.

And there were sons of Names. I never got as far as Khrushchev's son, though I had friends who studied with him and kept promising me. They really couldn't see why I should want to meet him—the personal lives of famous people arouse no curiosity, and anyway Sergei Khrushchev was *nye interesniy*. He was stodgy, they said, and no fun. But *interesniy* children of Supreme Soviet deputies, or other high-ups, were all over the place. I ran into the son of Peter Kapitsa, the physicist alleged to be largely behind the sputniks. His son, a glacologist, had just come back from exploring in the Antarctic with the Soviet expedition. And the son of Sergei Yesenin—recognized now in the USSR as being probably the greatest poet of the Soviet era. This son was a brilliant mathematician, and as a further example of how perfectly possible it is in Russia to learn a foreign language without being able to speak a word of it, he had actually translated English books—technical work on the most extraordinary learned level—although he could barely communicate anything verbally.

So there they are, even then only a small segment. If I learned nothing more about the Russians, I did begin to understand what diversity there was, what amazing extremes, what turmoil and ferment. I could make few generalizations about them as people, except from those aspects of their character which were essentially Russian. Russianness is something wonderful to me, but some Westerners have been known to disagree. I love them for their humanity—for the fact that they have retained a direct and real approach to life that many Westerners seem somehow to have forgotten. I love their incredible lack of artifice—or at least hopeless inability to put artifice over, their gregariousness, their warm hearts, their capacity for being very happy and very sad—to have a gloriously zany time or a huge mope, but almost always to cling to extremes. Even their carelessness and untidyness was appealing, their almost intentional bad manners and unconcern. None of this has any relation to things Soviet; on the contrary, the government is hopefully trying to discourage the more feckless aspects of the Russian character. But in general I found little response among ordinary people to the 'correct Soviet view' that was continually being prodded into them. As far as I could see, the Soviet gloss was still too new to include many major character upheavals or fundamental changes of outlook, Lysenko notwithstanding. Some Western observers think it has. The standard criticism that I object to most is the one about the Russians under the Soviet régime being nothing but a conforming mass of identical samenesses. In fact I sometimes wondered if they were possibly less conformist than Americans, for instance, because the majority of Americans *want* to conform and lose their identity. The American people detest individual aberrations; the Russian people admire them, with the governments of both countries often seeming to encourage the opposite state of affairs. The Russians do blend into the crowd superficially, because of a centuries-old fear of the results from above if they expose their individuality;

this seemed practically an automatic response, and most of those I met were something else again under their public façade. In fact they represented such diversity that it was difficult for me to cancel them out against each other and find a dominant pattern.

I have already explained that I went to the Soviet Union with little idea of what I would find, but nevertheless automatically felt at the beginning that one of the extremes to which I had been exposed would be confirmed. With this in mind I spent some time seeking to unravel the confusion of the ping-pong game. Somehow, inevitably, I thought, one of the two sides would predominate and I would see clearly what kind of place it was. Wonderful or horrible. This, I suppose, was mainly tied up to political conceptions, because I, like most people, thought first of a system of government when I thought of Russia. Not until I disregarded political confusions in favour of ordinary living confusions did I understand anything. What I understood then was that Moscow is a place to live. That's the first thing it is, the important thing. Its people are preoccupied with the same problems as Londoners or New Yorkers, and they are really very much the same in very many respects. They aren't a different breed of animal. Most of them don't feel particularly crushed because they live under dictatorship, nor particularly liberated because they live under socialism. They have a different conception of the future: that is the only major thing that is distinct among them all.

Perhaps I would have been able to confirm one of the extremes had I gone with a position, because it would have been easy to find evidence in support of anything. You find what you go looking for, as was proved to me most clearly by the members of the China delegation. Those who hated China found plenty to feed and sustain their hate; those who loved it saw no wrong. As with any situation, I believe their prejudices invalidate the deductions of many who go to Russia and then assemble lengthy one-sided masterpieces. It is carried right down the line by their audiences as well, who select that version which best supports their preconceived notions and carefully avoid references to another argument. How can it be that way? It isn't. In the first place, one cannot judge any situation with other values than the ones produced by the situation itself. I made that mistake at the beginning, often enough, and condemned on the basis of those aspects of Soviet life which appalled and revolted me and my standards. The second thing is that there are elements of everything existing there. I saw bad: the power motive and its abuses, the 'new class', the halt in cultural development in those areas where it is effectively controlled, and more. I lived with the symptoms of these things, with fear, inertia, hypocrisy, intolerance. And I saw good: a people given what they prize most—knowledge—and forever thirsting for more, a people with almost no economic insecurity, with equality of opportunity on the largest existing scale, and the staggering speed of progress in economy, science, industry and education, in this country so very recently backward. The results of these, too, were everywhere: courage for one, vitality, devotion, and a good deal of honesty. The opposites of bad and good blend, act, and react, in such overwhelming complexity that nothing is simple.

The main thing that I had to keep remembering about the people was that no one under the age of sixty knows any other kind of life. It is elementary, but easy to forget. It never occurs to them to see themselves as we see them, or to consider their system as something in doubt. It simply *is*. Although I have described people who do reconsider the basic ideas responsible for their way of life, most are no more like that than the ordinary people of any country. Proportionally, I haven't done very well on the side of the millions of normal, well-adjusted Muscovites. The average man is aloof from the world-shaking events around him, he would really rather not think about them, and he certainly wouldn't consider interfering with them. He would like peace, he would like to study and read, and he would like a nicer flat and clothes. He is proud of his country—and he really feels that it is his—he has more and more confidence in it, and, without rending his soul apart delving into economic theory, he believes that its system is the best, and that it is historically inevitable that the rest of the world will eventually follow a similar road. At the same time, although he is sure of the system's superiority, he often bitterly resents its abuses and excesses; he expresses his resentment by moaning and groaning, never with the idea that he himself is capable of effecting changes, but just to show that he isn't taking it all sitting down. However, now that he is aware of the crimes of Stalin, he would almost certainly do more than moan and groan if they were ever repeated. In any case, young people are being educated, and it would take a very powerful force indeed to regiment them as completely as their more ignorant parents were regimented.

There are, of course, real dissenting voices. The Shuras wouldn't hesitate to sacrifice their lives to make Russia a replica of America. They haven't a hope, but on the other hand they are learning that they can speak out more and more freely without consequences, and although many of their views are as distorted as those of people aggressively in favour, a great deal of their criticism is justified. They can speak now, they will continue to scream out their indignation more and more, people are going to listen ('The word has wings, the earth has ears'), and they will learn the effectiveness of their mass voice. Things can change as a result, even as they are now, and eventually the changes may be sufficient either for Shura to be able to go to America or for him to stop wanting to. Other things can make patterns shift: inevitably more people will become educated, more will think, and people's material lives will improve when less is required for basic industrial development. All these things are likely to lead in a hopeful direction. This is the happy side of the picture, and the one I feel will develop if the present trends are followed through. There are also unhappy alternatives, always possible as long as there is one power and no choice. But I cannot prophesy, nor have I any right to try.

The people I knew wouldn't or couldn't come to the West, but when they do they may find many surprises. Most of them have as false a picture of us as we have of them. The ones with visions of perfection would learn about our mistakes, the mistakes we forget in our attempt to create unity by concentrating so hard on theirs. Like many Russians with themselves, we deny we have faults; in the course of defending ourselves from outsiders we become so blind that we can justify almost anything. The Russians with the Dickensian picture would find much good that they could never have imagined existed. The Russian grumblers-about-little-things would, most unexpectedly, find their counterparts in Western society. But everyone would get a surprise, and that surprise is what is most needed today, on both sides. Each, now, has an entirely artificial idea of what the other side is like. Neither can accept friendly criticism, and each makes wild pronouncements about the other because of ignorance. In fact, our worst enemy is not the other side, but our own intolerance. If we want peace, which now means the survival of the world, no less, we must recognize truth—about ourselves and about others. The future existence of mankind may well depend on attitudes. Fear is so prevalent among all peoples that one can only wonder at the fantastic stupidity of the world—a world in which the majority, whatever their ideology, want love, and allow the opposite. More and more, after seeing how well people can get on together, I feel that the future should be shaped at the lowest level—us—instead of the highest. I could never hate the Russians now because I have met them and seen them as people in three dimensions, not just distorted figures in newspaper columns. You cannot hate when you understand, so why can't there be more of an attempt at understanding? Why need there be barriers between us?

Stranger, if you passing meet me and desire to speak to me,
*   why should you not speak to me?*
And why should I not speak to you?